M000209346

HEAL YOURSELF
with
ANGELS

About the Author

Patricia Papps (Dorset, UK) has studied angels and practiced meditation and spiritual healing for over twenty-five years. She is also an illustrator and has produced children's books, magazine illustrations, greetings cards, and stationery.

HEAL YOURSELF
with
ANGELS

Meditations,

Prayers,

and

Guidance

PATRICIA PAPPS

Llewellyn Publications
Woodbury, Minnesota

Heal Yourself with Angels: Meditations, Prayers, and Guidance © 2014 by Patricia Papps. All rights reserved. No part of this book may be used or reproduced in any manner whatsoever, including Internet usage, without written permission from Llewellyn Publications, except in the case of brief quotations embodied in critical articles and reviews.

FIRST EDITION
First Printing, 2014

Book design by Donna Burch
Cover art iStockphoto.com / 13274313 / Roman Okopny
Cover design by Kevin R. Brown and Gavin Duffy
Editing by Andrea Neff

Llewellyn Publications is a registered trademark of Llewellyn Worldwide Ltd.

Library of Congress Cataloging-in-Publication Data
Papps, Patricia.
  Heal yourself with angels : meditations, prayers, and guidance / by
Patricia Papps. — First Edition.
     pages cm
  ISBN 978-0-7387-3703-4
1. Angels. 2. Healing—Religious aspects. I. Title.
  BL477.P37 2014
  202'.15—dc23

                                                    2013038924

Llewellyn Worldwide Ltd. does not participate in, endorse, or have any authority or responsibility concerning private business transactions between our authors and the public.

All mail addressed to the author is forwarded but the publisher cannot, unless specifically instructed by the author, give out an address or phone number.

Any Internet references contained in this work are current at publication time, but the publisher cannot guarantee that a specific location will continue to be maintained. Please refer to the publisher's website for links to authors' websites and other sources.

Llewellyn Publications
A Division of Llewellyn Worldwide Ltd.
2143 Wooddale Drive
Woodbury, MN 55125-2989
www.llewellyn.com

Printed in the United States of America

DEDICATION

For Andrew, with love

CONTENTS

Introduction

By becoming more aware of the influence of angels in our daily lives, we become more aware of our spiritual self, a part of us that can bring deep peace and joy, for it connects us to Heaven. This can bring us the fulfillment and peace we search for and the realization that material things cannot bridge the gap between the desires of earth and the joys of Heaven.

The daily meditations detailed in this book will help you become attuned to angel energy as you go about your daily life. It is a beautiful energy that can inspire and work miracles to make your life happier and more joyful, for this is the role of the angels: to support humankind through the trials and tribulations of their earthly lives.

Working with angels in this way will bring a new dimension of love and joy to your life. The meditations are designed to bring much-needed healing, comfort, and inspiration to humanity and healing to the environment and to bring personal healing on a deep level. Working in this way with angels will lead you to a deeper understanding of your true self and the spiritual nature of all humankind.

Angels appear in all major religions of the world. This gives them a very "religious" aspect, which can be off-putting for some people. But angels have no religion. Indeed, their love and guidance are given freely to every human being on earth, regardless of the religious beliefs of the person. You don't need to be religious to work with angels, for everyone can feel their soft touch and hear their words of wisdom. Everyone can receive angel messages and experience their healing power in their lives. For the sake of ease, I have used the term "the Divine" in relation to a higher power in this book, but you can substitute your own name for a higher power when working with angels.

Angels are messengers of the Divine, and as such their message is for every single human being on earth and is one of love and joy, for their wish is for us to know the joy of Heaven during our lives on earth.

Our vision of angels is largely influenced by Renaissance artists who painted magnificent beings with glorious wings, no doubt giving them the ability to fly between Heaven and earth. This gives the impression that Heaven is a long way off and angels have to fly a great distance to reach us.

This is just not so, for angels exist on the ethereal planes, a sphere of life that is very close to our own; some would say that it is interconnected with our own world. Angels bring us the truth that Heaven is not a far-off place to be reached through good behavior and the correct religious beliefs, but rather is a state of being within ourselves. It is this truth that angels bring to us through their endeavors to lift us above the everyday aspects of our lives and reveal to us another way of looking at life.

Angels do not have a particular form, as human beings do, but are made of energy, for they vibrate at a much higher level than we do. Their light is the light of pure energy and love. This does not mean that angels are insubstantial in any way. Indeed, they are very strong and powerful beings with the ability to manifest in our world when necessary.

There have been many angel experiences recorded, especially over the last hundred years or so, for as humankind has moved toward the New Age of Aquarius, human consciousness has expanded, resulting in a deeper understanding and awareness of the angelic realms. As our consciousness has expanded, so have angels been able to come closer to bring their message of divine love and support that can heal our troubles and bring light where there is darkness in our lives.

I have worked with angels for many years and know the magic and miracles they can bring to one's life. Working with angels is a particularly satisfying part of my life and brings soul contentment and spiritual growth in the most beautiful of ways. Working with angels will bring to you a great sense of personal achievement and joy. Angels reveal to us our true potential and show us a magical path to follow in life—a pathway where you are accompanied by angels every moment of your life.

Chapter 1

WORKING WITH ANGELS

There is nothing mystical about working with angels, for they are always right beside us every minute of every day and they are only too happy to help us. In fact, they help us all the time without our asking, but we usually fail to notice and regard something good happening to us as just "good luck." However, focusing on a specific problem and concentrating on an appropriate angel will bring powerful guidance and help from the angel concerned. Your active involvement in the healing process will enable the angels to concentrate their efforts more accurately and powerfully.

Angels bring magic into our lives and can work miracles to make things right when things go wrong. They can sort out our most difficult problems and bring healing and harmony where there is disharmony and distress. They bring comfort where there is sorrow and bring their unconditional love to uplift us, regardless of how many mistakes we feel we have made in life. They are always by our side to bring help and inspiration when needed.

Working with individuals to bring divine love and wisdom into the world gives the angels particular joy. It is the angels' wish to work with human beings in this way. Their healing balm will resolve difficulties in your life and aid healing in the world where there is hardship, conflict, and despair.

We can greatly assist the angels in their work on our behalf by tuning in to their power, for their power is on the ethereal planes and we can provide a link from the ethereal to the denser matter of earth. We can help channel the angel light wherever it is needed on earth and, by being on earth ourselves, give greater power to that light. It is the purpose of our lives to work with angels and partner with them in their work of bringing divine love and wisdom to all of humankind. This is the work that our spirit yearns for and that can bring us the greatest satisfaction and reward.

Whatever the problem, and however big and difficult it may seem, angels can give us the ability to deal with it and move on. Solutions can easily be found to problems that appear insurmountable with the help of angels. Their soft touch of support and words of wisdom bring inspiration and upliftment when we are feeling down and out of our depth. If circumstances seem difficult, angel healing can help us regain control of our lives and pass through the difficulties with ease.

However you visualize angels, they are always positive energies who have the welfare of all humankind, the earth, and all living creatures as their sole purpose of being. Acknowledging their existence and the work they do for humankind can open the door to a wonderful creative relationship that will bring a deep happiness and fulfillment to your life. They work tirelessly behind the scenes wherever there is disharmony on a personal as well as a global level, and constantly send guidance to us to enable us to live happy and fulfilling lives. But we are often too busy and distracted by the material world to be aware of angel presence and guidance. When we "switch off" our ego and allow our spiritual self to make contact with angels, the results can be amazing and life-changing. Awareness of angelic help in any given situation will give that help extra potency because we are opening a direct channel to allow the angels' power to flow through.

The angels' purpose as messengers is to reveal to each one of us the truth that we are perfect beings of great power and that there is nothing to fear in life, for we are divinely guided and supported by angels every moment of our lives. Angels view all of humankind as beautiful spiritual beings and do not sit in judgment of any of us. They understand how dense the matter of earth is and how easy it is for us to become negative when trying to deal with everyday living. This is the message that angels bring, and their love, guidance, and support are the love, guidance, and support of the Divine.

Angels wish for us to view them as friends who are totally nonjudgmental of our failings and weaknesses and are only too ready to assist us to grow and prosper in life. Their magic can make our dreams come true and make our lives so much happier. This is a wonderful truth to keep in mind as we go about our daily lives. Angel messages are always inspirational, positive, and full of hope.

Angel healing works on our emotional and mental bodies to bring a deeper understanding of our spiritual selves. By helping to put us in touch with our spiritual selves, angels can bring us a deep peace and knowledge that all is well in our lives.

Angel healing will put us in touch with our *higher self* (as opposed to the *lower self* of everyday life), the core of our being that holds all the answers to the questions we have about our lives. This higher self holds the secrets of our true path in life, a path that can bring only happiness and joy. It is these secrets of our inner being that the angels can reveal to us, for they know everything about us, good and not so good, and they know the path we should be taking to attain this divine joy.

Angels know our true selves better than we do and understand the fears and lack of confidence that can lead us down a negative path. Angels gently steer us away from these negative patterns and put us in touch with our true, positive selves that can bring us to a happy pathway in life.

When working with angels, it is important to remember that they cannot interfere with our karma, but they can certainly make things easier and less painful for us. Karma is the law of cause and effect, which means we reap what we sow. Our karma gives us opportunities to grow and learn, and there is good and positive karma as well as so-called negative karma. Working with angels and allowing their love and wisdom to enter our lives can turn any negative karma we may have into positive opportunities, and the angels are always with us to help us work through problems.

If you are going through a difficult time or have what seems to be an insurmountable problem, there is an angel who can help you through it. By working with angels, you will overcome your problems with the greatest of ease. Karma is not a negative law, and in no way should it be seen as punishment for previous so-called sins. We always act to the best of our ability and knowledge at any given time, and the law of karma helps us to understand ourselves and to learn and grow spiritually.

The meditations detailed in this book will bring the angels to your side to share their wisdom and healing love with you with the most surprising results. Whatever your problem may be, there is an angel who will pour healing balm upon it and bring inspiration and upliftment to your life. However upset you may feel about something, there is an angel only too ready to enfold you in wings of love and light, bringing comfort and healing joy to your heart. Whenever I feel upset about something, I imagine myself enfolded in the wings of my Guardian Angel and I immediately feel uplifted and can almost hear the words of wisdom the angel is bringing to me about the situation. The daily meditations in this book will help you become very attuned to angel energy as you go about your daily life. This is a beautiful energy that can inspire you and work miracles to make your life happier and more joyful.

To begin this wonderful and creative journey of working with angels, you need only dedicate as little as ten minutes a day to making contact with them. Enjoy your work with them, for it is the wish of all angels to bring joy and happiness to every soul on earth through their healing and guidance.

Chapter 2

CONTACTING ANGELS

To contact an angel, all you have to do is visualize an angelic form or say the name of the angel you wish to contact and the relevant angel will be by your side to listen to your problem and give help where needed. It is as simple as that. Angels know what we need before we ask, so there is no need to give them a lengthy explanation as to why we need their help or what we are feeling. They support us through our difficulties, and this comfort can be experienced tenfold when we make the effort to make contact with them and give them our love in return.

You can contact angels anytime, anyplace, by simply being still for a few minutes and closing off your mind to the distractions of your environment. You just need to visualize an angel or try to be aware of angelic presence and the angels will be there by your side. Whatever your problem or difficulty in life, angels will be able to ease and support you through it. By attuning yourself to their presence, you will become accustomed to receiving messages from them as to the best way to proceed or the most suitable action to take.

It is important to remember, though, that angels are not our servants but are in the service of the Divine. They cannot do our bidding, particularly if our wishes have a negative aspect, but angel involvement will gently bring us to a position of understanding and acceptance of a course of action that will benefit all concerned. Angels can and do work miracles in our lives, so always be open to their power and work on any inspiration that comes to you. You will know it is angel inspiration, for it will give you a good feeling in your solar plexus and be very positive in outlook.

Meditation is a powerful and beautiful way to contact and work with angels. The meditations presented in this book are like silent prayers, for meditation focuses the mind and utilizes the great power of the mind not only to heal your own life but also to send healing into the world to heal individual pain, conflicts, and disharmony. Meditation stills the mind and emotions, bringing you into clear contact with your spiritual self, which is far more on the same "wavelength" with angels. Meditation with angels brings us a deeper knowledge of our true needs and helps to resolve problems of everyday living that stand in the way of us leading really happy and fulfilling lives.

The meditations in this book are simple to perform and require only a little concentration and the ability to visualize an angelic form and light. The angelic form you choose to visualize can be anything you feel comfortable with. It could be a great being of light or a more conventional image of an angel. The angel can be male or female—whichever feels most comfortable to you. How a person visualizes angels is a very personal thing. You may start with a conventional image of a winged being, and this could develop and change as you work with angels. It is very interesting to compare the image a person starts with to the image the person has, say, after working with angels for a few weeks.

The angels will know immediately that you are making contact with them and will be by your side to give you their love and support. At the beginning of each meditation is a short prayer to focus your mind on the angel to whom you are attuning yourself. All the angels in this book have a generic name or, in the case of the archangels, an individual name.

HOW TO MEDITATE: RELAXATION EXERCISE

To meditate, all you need to do is switch off your mind, relax, and concentrate on a visual image or thought. Stilling the mind in this way brings you into contact with your spiritual self and makes you realize that you are so much more than just the ego of everyday life.

Always start by relaxing yourself as detailed here, and choose a time of day when you feel most relaxed and when the cares of the day are least on your mind. This may be first thing in the morning before you start your day, or it may be in the evening when the tasks of the day are over. Choose somewhere comfortable to sit, and make sure you are not going to be disturbed. Later in this chapter I give suggestions for making an angel altar, which can be used with meditation. An altar focuses the mind and reminds you of the sacred nature of the task you are about to undertake. You may also like to light a candle and focus on the flame for a few moments, as this is a very good way of stilling the mind in preparation for meditation. The flame of the candle also symbolizes the little spark within us that is part of the Divine.

Your posture is important, as it keeps you alert during meditation. When you still your mind, it is easy to fall asleep! Sit in a comfortable chair, and make sure your back is straight and you are not slumped. You may prefer to sit on the floor, and this is fine in whatever position is most comfortable, such as with legs crossed or in the lotus position. If crossing your legs is uncomfortable for you, sit with your legs straight out in front of you. If sitting in a chair, have both feet firmly on the ground, although you can cross your feet if that is more comfortable. Make sure your back is straight, especially if sitting on the floor, and hold your hands loosely in your lap. It is important to be warm during meditation, so, if necessary, wrap yourself in a blanket.

Steady your breathing by taking some slow, deep breaths. Close your eyes and relax by becoming aware of your body. Are your shoulders relaxed? Very often the shoulders hold the most tension by being hunched nearly to one's ears. It is surprising how this happens without a person being at all aware of it. Let your shoulders drop and relax your arms. Then focus your attention on the rest of your body. Check for tension throughout your body, starting with your feet and working upward through your legs, abdomen, chest, neck, and head. The face can hold a lot of tension without a person realizing it, so make a conscious effort to relax your features. You might be surprised at how much tension your face holds. When you have done this exercise a few times, you will find you are able to totally relax yourself in less than a minute.

CREATING AN INNER TEMPLE

It aids the dynamics of meditation to have an *inner temple* in which you imagine yourself while meditating. Creating an inner temple prepares and focuses the mind very sharply in readiness for the meditation you are about to perform. This can be a fun exercise to do and will provide you with a safe and focused place in which to perform your meditation. In this exercise, simply use your imagination to create a temple in which you feel happy and at one with your spiritual self. The basis of this exercise can be used in conjunction with the more detailed meditations outlined in later chapters.

Sit in a comfortable position either in a chair or on the floor. Make sure that you are warm and that you will not be disturbed. Prepare yourself for meditation by relaxing as detailed in the previous exercise, then imagine yourself walking along a path in a beautiful countryside. The sky is a clear light blue and there is soft grass beneath your feet. Birds are singing and the sun shines warmly upon you. Ahead you see a building made of light. It shines and sparkles in the sunlight and looks very inviting. You walk up to the door at the front of the building and step inside. You immediately feel very safe and at home in this place. Look around and imagine how you would like your temple to be. Imagine the walls and ceiling. They sparkle with light. Perhaps your temple has a domed roof. Is can be either large or small. I find that a small temple is cozier, but that is only my preference.

The color of your temple is important. The walls could be a relaxing color, such as a pale blue or green. Yellow will bring a feeling of sunshine and warmth to your temple. Pink walls will bring a feeling of love, or you may prefer the relaxing and friendly color lilac. Walls and ceiling that are made of pure white light will bring extra purity and clarity to your work. Whatever color your temple is, it should glow with a beautiful light and give an overall feeling of safety and security. Are there windows? My temple has windows high up, through which streams sunshine, illuminating the spot where I sit. You feel very happy and relaxed in your temple.

You can have an altar to sit in front of, but this is not necessary. If you do have an altar, make it a simple one, perhaps reflecting your actual altar. (Details for making an angel altar are given later in this chapter.) If you usually sit on a chair to meditate, imagine a chair in your temple. If you usually sit on the floor to meditate, it is best to visualize yourself sitting on the floor of your temple. Imagine the floor as being made of colored tiles, and if you are sitting on the floor, it may be a good idea to imagine yourself sitting on cushions. Also imagine your temple as being very warm and comforting.

As you sit in your temple, you see standing before you a beautiful golden angel. This angel holds out his or her arms in welcome. Feel yourself surrounded by a warm, golden light that makes you feel very safe and happy. The angel enfolds you with a great love that brings peace to your heart and mind. The angel blesses your temple with the beautiful golden light and brings to your heart the knowledge that all is well in your life and that angels walk with you every moment of every day.

Sit here a while with this loving angel for as long as you feel comfortable. Then, when you feel ready, bring your awareness back to your actual surroundings and take a few deep breaths.

CLOSING DOWN YOUR CHAKRAS

After meditation, it is essential that you close down your chakras. Chakras are energy centers in the ethereal body that relate to different aspects of your being. There are seven chakras in total. Six are aligned along the spine, and the seventh is situated on the crown of the head. These chakras are activated when we are progressing along the spiritual path and also when we meditate. They spin with energy and light. As we become more spiritually aware, it is possible to actually feel the chakras spinning, especially the solar plexus chakra.

The first chakra is at the base of the spine and is associated with our instincts, those instincts that are essential to our survival and development in the material world. The second chakra is situated in the middle of the back at waist level. This chakra is associated with our feelings relating to our relationships and social standing. The third chakra is situated at the solar plexus and is very much concerned with our emotions and awareness. We have all felt that knot in the stomach at times of extreme stress. Fear and anxiety reside in the solar plexus, as do most negative emotions. We also get good feelings about things in our solar plexus, and if life is going well, we have a warm feeling in this area. The solar plexus is a good barometer of how things are going in our life.

The fourth chakra is at the heart center and is where we feel love and compassion. It is situated at the heart in the center of the chest. When we really feel good about something, we often can feel our heart center almost expanding in our chest. The fifth chakra is situated in the throat area and is associated with self-confidence and our ability to express our feelings and thoughts. When we feel stuck, the energy in this chakra can be affected and we may feel that we have something stuck in our throat.

The sixth chakra is our "third eye," or brow center, and is situated between the eyebrows. It is associated with our intuition and insight. This chakra is activated when we are developing our psychic abilities. The seventh chakra is situated on the crown on the head and is activated when one has reached a state of union with the Divine. It is often depicted as a thousand-petaled lotus.

It is very important after a meditation, however short, to close down your chakras for your protection. The chakras open during meditation to absorb the light and goodness and wisdom that the angels impart to you. Closing the chakras also acts as a good "grounding" exercise, to bring your awareness fully back to your present circumstances.

Closing your chakras is very simple to do. Just visualize each chakra, starting at the base chakra and working upward to your crown chakra, and visualize a silver cross in a circle of white light over the relevant chakra for a few moments. This will also have the effect of grounding you after the meditation.

AN ANGEL MEDITATION

Here is a simple meditation to practice that focuses on angels and is the basis for all the more specific meditations later in this book. Sit comfortably and perform the relaxation exercise described earlier in this chapter. When you feel fully relaxed, take a few more deep breaths, then breathe normally. Imagine yourself in your own special temple, sitting on the floor or on a chair, and see before you a vision of an angel. It doesn't matter how the angel looks. It may be male or female, with or without wings, but the important thing is that it be a being of light, made of light and surrounded by a glorious light.

Take note of how the angel is attired. He or she may be dressed in a magnificent gown like those in Renaissance paintings, or the angel may be dressed in a simple shift. You may find that the vision comes to you of an angel attired in contemporary clothing. Angels project themselves in a form we can recognize and feel comfortable with, so they often appear to us in human form. It matters not how the angel appears, for this is your vision. The only important thing, as I have mentioned, is the light. Light emanates from the angel and enfolds you, bringing you a feeling of contentment and love and the knowledge that all is well in your world, all is as it should be, and with the help of angels you will easily overcome any issue.

If you have a specific problem you want help with, focus on it and ask the angel for help. It may be a good idea to think of something that represents the problem—an image, a person, a scene—that you can think about during the meditation. As I have mentioned, the angel will know exactly what has happened, so you don't need to go into great detail, and the angel will be only too happy to help. Feel yourself enfolded in the love of the angel and know that this love is bringing healing and inspiration to your soul. Feel the love of the angel radiating throughout your body and filling you with a wonderful feeling of happiness and joy. Know that angel healing is working for you to bring about a positive solution to your problems.

With angel help, problems can be resolved very smoothly and quickly. Angels also bring their nonjudgmental wisdom to you, so you will find yourself learning from any mistakes you have made. Problems will be solved for the good of all concerned, and you will find yourself a stronger person because of this.

Hold the image of the angel in your mind for a few minutes. The light from the angel enfolds you and floods your whole being, bringing wisdom where you need answers and direction, and healing where it is needed in your life and in your body. Hold this image for a few minutes or for as long as you feel comfortable, then thank the angel for his or her help. Send the angel your love for the work he or she does to help you. This can be done by sending a ray of light to the angel from your heart center, a ray of love, or you can say quietly to yourself, "My love to you, dear angel," whichever you feel most comfortable with.

Now bring your awareness back to your breathing and take a few deep breaths to really bring your awareness back to your surroundings. Close your chakras as detailed earlier in this chapter, and take a sip of water to truly ground yourself. When you are grounded, you are fully aware of your surroundings and your mind is back in the present moment. It is a good idea to have a glass of water handy, as water is good for grounding after meditation.

It is also a good idea to have a pen and notebook handy to jot down any ideas or inspiration that came to you during the meditation. Angel magic works very fast, and if you open yourself to angel guidance, expect to receive that guidance quickly! After the meditation, take a little time to relax and think about any problems you have, for ideas on how to deal with them may well come to you. Don't worry if no ideas come; ideas or answers may very well come over the next day or so.

This is the start of an exciting partnership and journey, a journey that will bring a deep peace to your soul and a sense of well-being to your life. Angels can and do work miracles in our lives, and they have healing abilities for when we are depressed and upset. Whatever the problem, ask for angel help and that help will be there, for angels will never let you down. Your life will take on new meaning, for angels bring us closer to our true selves, the spirit within that is covered by the everyday ego. When we are in touch with our spirit within, life will blossom into positive experiences and the angels will be there by our side as we enjoy the journey.

MAKING AN ANGEL ALTAR

An altar focuses your energy and prepares you for communicating with your chosen angel. The altar can be anything you want it to be and can be great fun to create. First decide whether you are going to have a permanent altar set aside in a special space or if it is going to be portable. Both types can contain the same things, but the most important element is a white cloth. This symbolizes purity and is the basis for any altar, whether permanent or portable.

Set up your permanent altar in a spot where you know it is least likely to be disturbed and will be kept private, something only you see and use. If you live alone, this will be a fairly easy thing to do, but if you have a partner, he or she needs to know of your intentions and be supportive of them. A corner of the bedroom is an ideal place for a permanent altar, for it will not be seen by strangers or friends or family who may not understand what it is about.

To create the altar, use a small table covered with a white cloth, or if you like to sit on the floor to meditate, place the white cloth on the floor. The useful thing about having a white cloth is that it can be rolled up and put away and used only when you need it, thereby creating a portable altar. Having established where your altar is going to be, decide what items you will put on it. A lot of positive power will build up around the altar. Having a portable altar will in no way diminish the power that surrounds it, for if you have a white cloth and always use the same one, the angelic power will build around that. It is the work you do that builds the power. With a portable altar, you can roll up the contents you place on the altar and keep everything together in a safe place.

Crystals are ideal items to be placed on your altar. Rose quartz is particularly relevant for its healing powers, but use any crystal or stone that you feel very attuned to. You can also place on your altar a picture of an angel that particularly appeals to you. Have some fun and place objects that have a special spiritual meaning for you. If your altar is a permanent one, you could place a vase of fresh flowers on it, or if it is portable, dried flowers would be ideal, for they can just be placed on the cloth without a vase. Whatever you place on your altar, don't make it too cluttered, for this could distract the mind. A few well-chosen objects are ideal.

A good meditation practice is to have a special candle holder and candle, for focusing on the flame helps still and focus the mind in a truly beautiful way. The flame of the candle also symbolizes the light that shines in our heart center, that light being the spark of the Divine.

Regular use of your altar will automatically calm the mind and prepare you for focusing on the meditation with your chosen angel. The mind likes regularity and will be prepared for meditation whenever you sit before your altar. The energy that builds up there will help you in your chosen work and become very noticeable after a relatively short time.

Chapter 3

HOW TO RECEIVE ANGEL MESSAGES

Angel messages can come to us in many different ways, for angels know no bounds when it comes to contacting us. They can be quite inventive in how they choose to communicate with us.

One of the most common ways for angels to contact us is for an idea or answer to just come into our head when we have turned off the daily chatter of our mind. It is a good idea to have an "angel communication" time each day when you still your mind and think about any problems or questions you may have. Then clear your mind of any thoughts and concentrate on the angel you are working with at the present moment. Relax and don't try too hard to receive messages, for this may block the communication. And don't worry if no answers or ideas come to you, for angels work in many ways and can give you messages when you least expect it. Ideas can come into your head at any time of the day, when your mind is completely involved with something else, so it's a good idea to carry a notebook and pencil with you at all times so you are ready to deal with the thoughts and ideas that come to you.

It is easy to recognize angel messages when they pop into your head, for you will have a good feeling about them, an almost *Why didn't I think of that before?* sort of feeling. The message will answer your question in a very sensible way, and you will know it is angel inspiration, for you will often get a surge of joy in your solar plexus or heart center.

Sometimes the messages or answers can come through other people, who may say something that is the answer you have been looking for. Other people are probably not aware that they are giving you angel messages. They just feel inspired to say something to you at that particular moment, and it is something that strikes a chord with you.

The best time to receive angel messages is during meditation, when the mind is totally focused on angel power and it is easier for the angel concerned to communicate with you. Let your mind go blank for a few minutes and relax. Focusing on a candle flame is a good way to relax and prepare the mind to receive messages. This technique has worked for me on numerous occasions when I needed answers to a problem.

Spontaneous writing is another way to receive angel messages. Just relax with a notepad and pen and let your mind go blank. Then think about the problem or question you need an angel response to, and hold your pen ready for writing. Write anything that comes into your mind, no matter what it is, and you will be surprised at what can emerge. Just let a spontaneous train of thought lead your hand in writing.

Emma, a friend of mine who works with angels on a regular basis, had a dilemma involving her work. She had a very good job with good prospects, but she was wondering whether to give that all up and do volunteer work abroad helping the poor. She was torn between the two and worried that if she went for the volunteer work, it would not turn out as she hoped.

Emma decided to stay with her current job, in which she was sure she was soon to get a promotion and an increase in salary, but just out of curiosity she decided to try spontaneous writing. She had been working with Archangel Uriel, who helps people find direction in life, and asked him if she had made the right decision. She got out her notebook and pen and prepared to write. She found, to her surprise, that she wrote, "Go for it, volunteer work," "Go for it, volunteer work," over and over again. She took this as a sign from the angels that she should pursue the volunteer work, which she did and found that it made her happier and more satisfied than she had ever felt in her whole life. She also worked with Archangel Michael to protect the weak and vulnerable, which brought an extra dimension to her life. She did not have any regrets and made lots of new friends and met her husband-to-be while working abroad. It was a truly life-changing choice.

Angela, another friend of mine, asked a question while meditating with the Throne angels on relationship issues. She was not sure of the current relationship she was in and had nagging doubts about whether it was right for her. She asked the Throne angel for guidance and meditated on the problem. She focused on a lighted candle and heard the words "end it" very clearly. She decided to trust in the angel's guidance and ended the relationship.

Some months later, Angela met up with a friend of hers who was now going out with her old boyfriend. This woman told Angela that it was an abusive relationship and that she was scared to end it for fear that he would become even more abusive. Angela felt relieved that she had ended the relationship when she did, or she could have ended up a victim as well. She suggested working with angels to her friend to help her find the courage to end the relationship. She thought perhaps her friend would think her silly to suggest such a thing, but the woman was very open to the idea. Angela suggested she work with the Throne angels to give her the courage to end the relationship and also work with the Cherubim angels for protection. The last Angela heard was that the friend was in a much happier relationship and had no further problems with her former abusive boyfriend.

Another example is my friend Amanda, who felt that her life was going nowhere and desperately needed to change, but couldn't make up her mind which way to go. She decided to work with Archangel Uriel to find some direction in her life, for she had several options. One was to go back to college to learn new skills, and another was to start her own business, though she didn't know what type of business to start. She felt daunted at the prospect of making such a major change in her life but knew she must move ahead and give up her job, which was a dead end and made her feel hopeless and drained of energy.

Amanda asked Archangel Uriel to give her some direction, and very soon she found herself feeling very good and excited about the idea of starting her own business. She didn't know what that business would be, so she asked Archangel Uriel for some ideas. The answer came to her quite suddenly when she was at work and not thinking of anything in particular. The word "flowers" suddenly popped into her head, and she knew immediately that it was the reply from Archangel Uriel. She loved flowers and flower arranging, and she knew then that her new venture would be that of a florist. She had a very good feeling in her solar plexus about the idea.

At first the idea seemed a little out of reach, as she did not have the capital needed to start such a business. But she believed in the angels and started meditating with Archangel Gabriel to help her make this major change in her life. He gave her the courage to take the first steps toward her goals, but she felt that acquiring a bank loan would not be possible. To her surprise, the bank manager was very supportive of the idea, and she got the loan she needed. She found a good location for her floral shop and took the final step of handing in her notice at work. She kept meditating with Archangel Gabriel and found that all went smoothly.

Soon after, to her delight, she had a very prosperous business and felt much more satisfied and happy with her life.

Angel help can come in many ways. Constance, an acquaintance of mine, found she was in need of such help when applying for a job. The new position was very important to her, but while driving to the interview she found herself lost after taking a wrong turn. Unfortunately, she did not have a map with her, so her written directions were useless. She stopped and asked a passer-by how to get to the building, but that person did not know. Time was running out, and she began to worry that she would miss the appointment.

Constance said a silent prayer to her Guardian Angel to help her and felt a strange sense of relief. She was about to stop to ask another pedestrian when a voice in her head told her to take a right turn. The voice continued to give her directions until she was back on the correct route and she knew where she was. She knew it was her Guardian Angel who had directed her and had come to her aid in her hour of need. After such a worrying time, she needed to relax and prepare for the interview, so she imagined herself in the loving wings and light of her Guardian Angel. She felt a renewed sense of confidence and handled the interview in a very positive way. When she got the job, she thanked her Guardian Angel for the support and help.

Another friend of mine was working with the Dominion angels on her inner wisdom and had asked them a question about her spiritual path. She waited nearly two weeks for an answer, and when it came, it was pretty dramatic. She was in a library when a book fell off a shelf she was passing and hit her on the head. When she picked up the book and looked at the page that was open, there was the answer to her question!

Not all replies from angels arrive in such a dramatic fashion, thank goodness, and hopefully your answers will come in a less flamboyant manner. But when the answers do come, always trust the guidance of angels, for they are never wrong. Have courage and take the course of action they advise, and you will find yourself experiencing hope and inspiration that will bring a newfound joy to your life.

Chapter 4

GUARDIAN ANGELS

We all have a Guardian Angel who is with us from our birth to our passing. The purpose of our lives is to ultimately find our true spiritual self, that heaven within us, that is a true spark of the Divine. This true spiritual self is found through the events of our lives, through our karma, and the purpose of our Guardian Angel is to guide us along the right path.

We all come into life with a "blueprint" of the course that our life should take to gain the maximum opportunity to realize the goal of achieving union with that spark of the Divine within. Christ said that we should seek heaven first and "all else will be added unto you." This means that working from the Divine within will bring untold happiness, contentment, and fulfillment and bring us the good fortune we so greatly desire in life. When working from the Divine within, nothing can go wrong and all mistakes and disappointments become achievements that bring great satisfaction to the soul. Through finding that divine spark within, we will feel really good about ourselves, which is half the battle to living a happy and successful life.

Our Guardian Angel knows all our needs and desires, all our so-called faults and the reasons for them. Guardian Angels are not here to judge us. Quite the contrary. They sympathize with our every mistake and with our despair, and joyously celebrate when we are happy or achieve something good. Our Guardian Angel knows how dense the layers of the earth life are that cover us and how vulnerable we are to negative feelings. Our ego, our earth self, is also very sensitive to the negativity of others, which can cause great distress in our lives. But our Guardian Angel tries to guide us along a path of positivity. We should not feel down or depressed if we think we have failed in some way, for all failure is but a learning curve from which we can learn valuable lessons and move toward our goal of achieving spiritual union with the Divine.

We all have a unique purpose to our lives, and our Guardian Angel helps steer us along the right pathway to achieve that purpose. Coincidences, being in the right place at the right time, a lucky meeting with someone who can help us—all these are the behind-the-scenes work of our Guardian Angel, who strives nonstop to ensure that we are given the greatest opportunity to achieve the purpose for which we came into this life.

Whenever we need help in our lives, when it seems that everything is going wrong, we just need to call on our Guardian Angel and the most loving and powerful help will be at hand. Our Guardian Angel will help us through life's difficulties and ease us through our karma, which can sometimes be difficult to deal with. It is wonderful to know that right beside us, in every moment of our lives, there is a powerful being who has unconditional love for us and is only too ready to help in any way. Guardian Angels do all they can to help us and bring us upliftment when we feel down. They help us stay positive when life gets tough, for it is all too easy to fall into negative thinking and feelings when things go wrong. But with the help of our Guardian Angel, we can keep a positive attitude that will enable us to move through situations that cause hurt. Guardian Angels are our comforters when we need reassurance and our loyal friends when we need someone to confide in. They are always there for us when we need some TLC.

When you have what seems to be an insurmountable problem, discussing it with your Guardian Angel can be a real help, for just talking it through can clarify the situation in your mind and help you to see the problem in a new light. Don't be afraid to ask for the assistance of your Guardian Angel, for no problem is too small for help to be given. When working with angels, you will be surprised at what can happen! Fresh insights and ideas will come to you that will help you solve the problem in a very positive way.

To receive angelic assistance, simply imagine this wonderful being and ask for the help you need. That help will be there for you, for your Guardian Angel will never let you down.

I feel very close to my Guardian Angel first thing in the morning, before I start the tasks of the day, and last thing before I go to bed at night, when I have switched off from the cares of the day. I also try to make contact during the day at some point to help me stay positive and at peace. At such times I have a few private moments with my Guardian Angel about what has happened during the day and my hopes and dreams for my life. It is beneficial to have some quiet time with your Guardian Angel to divulge your hopes and dreams. These will also serve as positive affirmations that will bring your dreams nearer to being a reality. You can do this anytime during the day when you feel relaxed and are alone. Just close your eyes and imagine a beautiful angel in front of you giving you his or her undivided attention and love and listening to every word you say.

If things are really going badly in your life and you feel down or unhappy about something, imagine the wings of your Guardian Angel enfolding you in all the love the angel has to offer. This is an incredible amount of love, and you will feel uplifted and cherished. I do this whenever I feel very down, and it always makes me feel better, for it is not my imagination but is very real. Your Guardian Angel really is there caring for you and wishing you well. If you are feeling really desperate about something and don't know which way to go, turn to your Guardian Angel and you will immediately feel better knowing that his or her wisdom will guide you through. Feel yourself enveloped in the angel's unconditional love, and you will feel comforted, empowered, and ready to face whatever challenges await you. Whenever I do this exercise, I can really feel myself surrounded with love, and I find I have renewed energy and courage to face my tasks with a hopeful heart.

Your Guardian Angel is always with you, unlike the other angels who come and go when you have need of their particular gifts. Even when you are meditating and communicating with the other angels in this book, your Guardian Angel is always with you to assist in the work you are undertaking with a particular angel. Your Guardian Angel will bring added power to help you achieve whatever you have set out to do, be it sending love and healing into the world or healing a relationship issue that is causing you pain. Your Guardian Angel is always with you to provide support and give you the confidence you need to successfully complete your goals. No matter how bad the situation is, your Guardian Angel will give you love and upliftment to help you cope.

When my father was terminally ill, I "saw" him surrounded by angels and knew that he would be all right and cared for with all the love the angels had to offer. I also held my mother in the light of the angels and knew that her Guardian Angel was giving her the courage to cope with a very sad and distressing situation.

To actually meet your Guardian Angel is an exciting experience. A simple meditation is all that is necessary to establish a bond between the two of you.

MEDITATION TO MEET
YOUR GUARDIAN ANGEL

Make yourself comfortable and warm. Make sure your back is straight, for this helps you to focus your attention on the meditation. Sit before your altar and do the relaxation exercise as detailed in chapter 2. You may also like to light a candle and focus on the flame for a few moments to help still the mind further. The little flame acts as a reminder of the divine spark within.

When you feel fully relaxed and focused, imagine that you are in a beautiful walled garden. The sun shines brightly and the garden is filled with flowers and trees. You feel warmed by the sunshine and at peace in these beautiful surroundings. There is an exquisite perfume in the air. You are seated under a tree in full blossom. Birds sing softly around you. The scene is very peaceful and idyllic.

On the opposite side of the garden there is a door in the wall. This door opens and a beautiful angel comes into the garden. This is your Guardian Angel. The angel comes toward you with arms outstretched in loving greeting. You get up and move toward the angel and allow yourself to be embraced in a wonderful feeling of love and joy. Then you sit down again and your angel stands before you. How you visualize this angel is entirely up to you.

The angel may be male or female, and dressed in traditional or contemporary clothing. He or she may have wings that are made of light. Your angel emits wonderful rays of light, rainbow colors of pure sparkling light that enfold you in a wonderful feeling of joy. Notice the predominant color of the light and the color your angel is dressed in, for this is quite significant. (We will discuss colors in depth in chapter 5.)

As the angel stands before you, you feel a wonderful feeling of warmth and love and know you are constantly protected by this great being. You know that you can be absolutely honest about your feelings on any matter that troubles you and that the angel will not stand in judgment of you. Quite the contrary. He or she will sympathize with you and be only too happy to help. The love you receive from your angel is totally unconditional and will never fail you. Feel this love as a warm glow that starts at your feet and works up through your entire body. You feel greatly at ease and more at peace with your life than ever before. You know that with this wonderful being at your side, you can overcome all obstacles and problems. The light of your angel will never diminish, and neither will his or her love. Nothing else exists at this moment but the light from the angel that enfolds you, and you know that whatever is happening in your life at this time, all will be well and you will move through it all with ease.

If there is anything in particular that you wish to discuss with your angel, you can do so now. You know that you have the undivided attention of your angel, and the angel will know all your true feelings about the matter and will do all in his or her power to help you. Just discussing the matter with the angel will help put it in a new perspective, and the love of your angel will give you insights and ideas on how to deal with and solve the problems.

Give the angel your love in return. You can do this by imagining a deep love at your heart center that manifests as a beautiful rose-colored light that enfolds your angel, or you can say, "My love to you, dear angel," whichever you feel most comfortable with. Thank your angel for being with you and for the help and power that he or she offers to you.

Relax in the love and joy in which you are enfolded for as long as you feel comfortable. Then when you feel ready, bring your awareness back to your actual surroundings and concentrate on your breathing once more. Close down your chakras as detailed in chapter 2, then take a few sips of water to really ground yourself. Don't forget to put out your candle!

After you have made contact through meditation and feel a bond with your Guardian Angel, it is much easier to establish a link anywhere and anytime you need your own special angel to bring upliftment and help. Just be still and quiet for a few moments and imagine the beautiful angel standing in front of you or enfolding you in wings of love. You will feel the warmth of your angel's love and the joy this love brings to your heart. It is as simple as that to make contact with your Guardian Angel, for he or she is right beside you all the time sending love and positive energy to you every minute of every day.

As you go about your daily tasks, remember that you have a devoted friend of the angelic realms right beside you to give you the upliftment and strength to deal with all your work and problems as they arise. This is truly a wonderful reality, and to believe it and work with it makes life so much more enjoyable. Knowing you have this friend beside you means you can talk to him or her whenever you wish just by being silent for a few minutes and voicing your concerns or questions in your mind while imagining your angel. This is the start of a wonderful partnership that will bring joy and positivity to all aspects of your life.

Chapter 5

THE COLORS OF YOUR GUARDIAN ANGEL

The color in which your Guardian Angel appears to you is an indicator of what you are lacking or needing at the present moment. For instance, green is a cleansing color and may indicate that cleansing of some sort is necessary at this time. This may be cleansing of dis-ease of the body, such as an infection or other illness, or it may be cleansing of negative thoughts that go round and round in your mind. Whatever needs cleansing, a meditation with your Guardian Angel in this color will greatly relieve such problems and lift the negativity from your mind.

When meditating with your Guardian Angel, imagine yourself bathed in green light and feel it flowing throughout your entire being. This can be a very powerful meditation for cleansing unwanted thoughts or infections of any kind. I have found that it clears up viral infections very quickly. The next time you have a cold or a similar infection, try meditating with your Guardian Angel bathed in green. This can speed up the healing process and bring you a new vitality.

Green is also the color of harmony, and seeing your Guardian Angel bathed in a beautiful emerald-green light can indicate that you live your life in a very harmonious manner or that you need some harmony in your life. Disharmony can take many forms, one of which is not maintaining the right balance between work and leisure. If this is a problem for you, the meditation with the Cherubim angels in chapter 9 will help enormously by bringing you the wisdom to restore balance to your life.

If there is disharmony between you and someone else, be it a friend, partner, or work colleague, the meditation with the Throne angels in chapter 10 will be of great benefit to restore harmony to the relationship. Disharmony between ourselves and others can happen for many reasons, often because we feel under attack or criticized, or maybe a misunderstanding has caused distress. Throne angels will bring understanding and healing to such situations, indicating to you the best course of action to take to restore harmony.

Blue is a very peaceful color, and if your Guardian Angel comes to you bathed in blue light, this indicates a need for peace and tranquility in your life. It may be that you have a very hectic lifestyle and need to slow down a little. Meditating with your Guardian Angel and absorbing the blue light into your aura will help a great deal in finding peace and tranquility. The very act of meditating will bring a deep calm to your life and help you maintain that calm in all you do.

A Guardian Angel appearing to you bathed in blue light can mean the opposite in that you are someone who has found the deep peace of the spirit within and you lead a very happy life. Deep peace comes from accepting yourself and dealing with your faults in a positive manner. No one is perfect, but accepting ourselves as we are is a very difficult thing to do. We accept others with all their faults and are willing to forgive another person's irritating little habits, but that is often not the case with ourselves. We are only too ready to accuse ourselves and judge ourselves as guilty.

If you have found peace within, you are very advanced on the spiritual path, for accepting ourselves as we are is one of the biggest stumbling blocks to leading a happy and positive life. Meditating with your Guardian Angel enveloping you in blue light will bring you to that place of peace by encouraging you to forgive your faults and accept yourself unconditionally. You can also work with the Virtue angels to bring peace and harmony to the world, as described in chapter 13, for this peace and harmony will envelop your soul and bring a deep peace and fulfillment within.

Yellow light around your Guardian Angel indicates wisdom, and it may be that you are a soul with great wisdom or it may indicate that you need some wisdom in your life right now. Perhaps you have a problem that needs solving or a situation that is complicating your life, and a little wisdom would help sort it out. Meditate on your Guardian Angel radiating a yellow light and wait for answers and insights that will help you in your endeavors. Alternatively, meditate with the Dominion angels for inner wisdom, as detailed in chapter 11, for they will help you contact that spark of the Divine within that holds all the answers you need to lead a harmonious and happy life.

Yellow is also associated with courage or the lack of it, so maybe there is a situation in your life that fills you with dread and a feeling of not knowing which way to turn. Meditating with your Guardian Angel radiating the color yellow will bring courage to your soul and help you face any situation that is causing you difficulties and show you the way to deal with it and move on.

A Guardian Angel bathed in a rose-colored light indicates love. Perhaps you are a person with a lot of love to give, in which case you must be a very happy and contented person, for love is the most powerful of emotions, and, if given freely to everyone you know, must make for a very contented life. Practice the meditation with the angels as detailed in chapter 29, and send your love into the world with the love of the angels. This love brings healing where it is needed and brings hope where there is none. Love is a very powerful emotion, and sending it into the world brings help and healing to many who so badly need it. This is very uplifting and satisfying work to do and will bring untold joy to your heart if you share your love with humanity.

It may be that you are missing love in your life at the moment and are in need of some TLC. If that is the case, meditate with your Guardian Angel bathed in a beautiful rose-colored light and you will notice a great difference in your life. Imagine your Guardian Angel enveloping you in wings of love and comforting you, and you will feel much better and more positive. If love is lacking in your life, this meditation will attract loving people into your life or perhaps change the way your associates, family members, and friends react to you. Love also brings wisdom, so you may find you have ideas on how to change your attitude to attract love into your life. The meditation with the Throne angels in chapter 10 will also help resolve specific issues between yourself and others and will help diminish loneliness if this is something that particularly distresses you.

Gold is a powerful color and indicates warmth, positive energy, and wisdom. If your Guardian Angel is radiating a golden light, it indicates that you are a warm, positive person who has little problem dealing with the difficulties of life. You have found your true pathway and enjoy the satisfaction and enjoyment this brings.

Gold can also indicate that you need the power of gold in your life at present, for you have a negative attitude for some reason. Meditate with your Guardian Angel enfolding you in a glorious golden light and feel the warmth of this color radiating throughout your whole being. It will restore a positive attitude to life and bring clarity to your mental and emotional outlook and a warmth of being that will change your perception of life. The meditation with the Cherubim angels in chapter 9 will also have a very powerful effect on negative attitudes and bring positive energy where needed.

Gold is a very beneficial color if you are feeling depressed for some reason. Meditate with your Guardian Angel and feel yourself enfolded in a beautiful golden ray of love that completely wraps around you from your toes to your head. It will bring you the wisdom to understand why you are depressed and what you can do about it. This is a lovely color to meditate with on a winter's evening when you may be feeling a bit down, for the golden rays will bring the sunshine of summer to your soul and lift you up to face life with a new vigor. In fact, if you suffer from the winter blues, this is a good color to bathe yourself in to feel the positive upliftment of the golden sun. I suffered from the winter blues for several years before I started working with my Guardian Angel and the golden ray. It really helps lift me up and fills me with positive energy and happiness.

Should you have a serious problem with depression, meditation with the Archangel Jophiel, as described in chapter 27, can be very healing and uplifting. He is a powerful angel, and with the help of your Guardian Angel, Archangel Jophiel can really lift your spirits and bring about a wonderful healing, for depression is a serious illness. Always consult your doctor if you are seriously depressed, as there may be an underlying cause.

The color violet is associated with the higher self, so if your Guardian Angel comes to you bathed in violet light, it means that you are very close to that divine spark within. Violet indicates someone quite well developed on the spiritual path and means that you are making a determined effort to discover the Divine within you. Meditating with your Guardian Angel and the violet light will bring you closer to your goal and bring wisdom, courage, and altruistic love for all humankind and all creatures of the earth. This can only bring great happiness and joy, for to connect with the higher self within is to find, and live through, your true self, that spark within that is of the Divine. You will discover the truth of your being, which will bring everlasting contentment and a great deal of happiness in the service of others. The self, or ego, can finally be put aside, and the truth of your being can shine forth to heal and help where you find there is need. The meditations in this book that send love and healing into the world for specific problems will be especially satisfying work for you and will bring you the greatest happiness and joy and bring you closer still to the spark of the Divine within.

Violet is the color of healing, as Christ was the Great Healer, so if your Guardian Angel comes to you bathed in violet, it may be that you have healing powers. It will bring the greatest satisfaction to your soul to develop these powers and bring healing into the world on an individual and worldwide basis. Try working with the Archangel Raphael to send healing to those who need it, as detailed in chapter 20. This is very rewarding work and will develop your healing abilities.

If your Guardian Angel is bathed in orange or red light, this indicates that physical energy may be lacking in your life. Perhaps you are feeling run-down after an illness or after a particularly stressful time in your life and your energy is at a low ebb. It could also indicate a lack of exercise in your life that you are aware of but doing nothing about! Meditating with your Guardian Angel radiating a vibrant orange light will help restore balance to your energy level and bring about a beautiful healing to your body and mind.

Orange is the color of energy, so filling yourself with the orange light of your Guardian Angel can only rejuvenate your spirit and soul. When a person becomes run-down, it can be very difficult to get back to a normal energy level. Meditating with your Guardian Angel radiating an orange light can rebalance your energy and bring renewed vigor to your body. The meditation with the Cherubim angels in chapter 9 is also beneficial if you are experiencing a low energy level, for the Cherubim bring powerful healing and positive energy to the tired soul.

If your Guardian Angel comes to you bathed in a beautiful silver light, this indicates that you are taking the right path in life and progressing well on the spiritual path. Silver indicates spiritual progress, and meditating with your Guardian Angel bathed in silver will give you the wisdom and the help you need to grow spiritually. Working with the Powers angels to help combat evil in the world, as described in chapter 14, will bring great spiritual satisfaction and will help you grow in love and wisdom.

Silver is also an indicator of pain, whether physical or emotional, and is a very healing color in this respect. Whenever I have a sharp pain, such as discomfort due to indigestion or a muscular pain somewhere, I imagine a strong silver ray radiating from my Guardian Angel to the painful spot, and the pain usually goes away fairly quickly. Pain is an indicator that something is wrong, so I recommend that persistent pain be checked out by a doctor.

If you are suffering from emotional pain, then meditating with your Guardian Angel bathed in a strong silver light can help heal the hurts that are causing you such distress and bring you the wisdom to know how to deal with it. Emotional pain can be very difficult to deal with, for it sends negative thoughts into your mind that go round and round and only serve to make the pain worse. The mind finds it difficult to let go of the hurt and constantly goes over the situation that is to blame. The silver light of your Guardian Angel can heal this negative mental problem and bring healing to the hurt that is so depressing. If forgiveness is needed, your Guardian Angel can give you the strength and understanding to find this in your heart, for forgiveness is the only way to find true healing in such situations. Working with the Throne angels, as detailed in chapter 10, is also very powerful where forgiveness is necessary, for they in particular bring help where there is a relationship issue.

If your Guardian Angel comes to you bathed in pure white, this indicates a purity of heart and mind. It suggests that you are a very advanced soul who knows exactly where you are going in life. You feel sure of your way on the spiritual path, and this pathway brings you great fulfillment and joy. The practice of the meditations in this book that concentrate on sending harmony, healing, and love will bring a special satisfaction to the soul and help you advance further on your chosen pathway.

However, a Guardian Angel bathed in white can also mean the opposite and indicate confusion in your heart and mind about the correct spiritual path for you to take. If you meditate on your Guardian Angel dressed in white and enfolding you in a pure white light, your questions will be answered and your self-doubt will be healed. A new path will open before you, and you will finally feel that you have found the right way for you. Be open to signs and indications. These can come in many ways, such as being in a bookshop and finding a book that immediately resonates with you and shows you the way to go, or it may be a friend who opens your eyes to a new way of living. You will know you are going in the right direction because it will give you a good feeling—a feeling of satisfaction and excitement that you are on the right path at last.

The meditation with Archangel Chamuel in chapter 24 will help you if you are confused about your spiritual path, for his wisdom and love will bring clarity to muddled thoughts. He will give a clear indication of the best route for you to follow, for Archangel Chamuel helps where inner wisdom is needed. He will bring his clear guidance to bear upon your questions and confusion about the spiritual path that is right for you.

Guardian Angels may come bathed in several colors, for several issues may be relevant in your life at any given time. If your Guardian Angel comes to you with all the colors of the rainbow, don't be confused, for this means that you are a very balanced person, so you are obviously doing something right! It means you are sure of your pathway in life and have everything well balanced between work and rest, material and spiritual.

As with all colors, the opposite can also be true. If this is the case here, then spend some time meditating on your Guardian Angel bathed in the colors of the rainbow to get your life more evenly balanced. You must be feeling pretty stressed out, so achieving a balance between work and relaxation is very important. Try meditating with your Guardian Angel radiating a green light, for this is the color of harmony and will give you the wisdom to rebalance your life. Meditating with the Cherubim, as detailed in chapter 9, will also greatly help in restoring the balance between work and leisure, thereby restoring your energy level and equilibrium of mind, body, and spirit.

Whatever your problem, your Guardian Angel is there for you at any time of the day. He or she will never abandon you and is only too willing to bring his or her magic to influence your life. This magic can be truly wondrous and healing. To have a friend in whom you can confide anything is a wonderful gift and will make life joyful and inspiring. When you feel down, confused, or at a loss as to the right way to turn, imagine yourself enveloped in the wings of your Guardian Angel and you will feel yourself uplifted by the most powerful love—a love that will bring you new enthusiasm for life and clarity of mind as to the right decisions to make. It is really wonderful to have such a friend who can work true magic in your life.

Chapter 6

HIERARCHIES OF ANGELS

Angels are organized into hierarchies, which are subdivided into choirs. Each choir of angels has a different task to perform. Hierarchical status is not important to angels, for all angels perform the work of God and have the good of humankind and the earth as their sole purpose of being.

Over the centuries, humankind has given varying degrees of importance to the angels, and we have given some angels superior roles, which makes them seem very distant from us. But all angels are humble and regard all the work they do as being of equal importance. It is important to remember this when working with angels, for it is easy to feel overwhelmed by the so-called importance of angels, such as perhaps the Seraphim angels. But the Seraphim are only too happy to take the opportunity to work directly with humankind in an equal partnership and don't regard themselves as any more important than the angel who looks after a little wildflower.

In the seventh century CE, Pope Gregory the Great proclaimed that there were nine "orders of angels," each with a different task to perform. These nine orders, known as choirs, are divided into three hierarchies, each with three choirs. The following is a brief list that can be used as a guide to the angel you wish to work with at a particular time.

FIRST HIERARCHY, FIRST CHOIR

Seraphim Angels

The Seraphim give all their love and support to humankind when there is some sort of disaster, whether human-made or natural. Their power is with rescue workers and victims alike, and to tune in to the Seraphim during times of disaster can greatly focus and direct the power of these angels where it is needed most. This is a beautiful way to assist the Seraphim angels in their healing work.

FIRST HIERARCHY,
SECOND CHOIR

Cherubim Angels

The Cherubim are concerned with positive energy, and meditation with them can help bring some "zing" back into our lives if we are run-down, perhaps due to overwork or illness. The Cherubim also help when we are stressed and tired by restoring energy and bringing wisdom to reorganize our busy working days. Lethargy is also helped by the Cherubim, who revitalize the negative thought patterns that can lead to lethargy and a "What's the use?" attitude to life.

FIRST HIERARCHY,
THIRD CHOIR

Throne Angels

Thrones support us with any problems we have regarding relationships or loneliness. Meditation with the Throne angels will greatly help to resolve any difficulties or disharmony that exists between ourselves and another person, be it a partner, friend, work colleague, or family member. Thrones also assist us if we feel lonely by helping us attract like-minded people into our lives.

Second Hierarchy, Fourth Choir

Dominion Angels

Dominion angels remind us that we are spiritual beings and that our purpose on earth is to find our true spiritual self. Our true selves bring altruistic love for all humankind, which we can send out into the world for the good of all. Finding our true spiritual self can bring us the greatest joy and peace, for we know that all is well in our lives, and life's problems melt away or become easier to deal with when seen in the light of the spirit.

Second Hierarchy, Fifth Choir

Virtue Angels

Virtue angels are very much concerned with environmental issues and looking after the earth. They bring the light of wisdom to those in positions of power in the world to heighten their awareness of protecting the environment. They also help all organizations and individuals whose work focuses on green issues and the care of our planet. Virtue angels have the whole earth in their care, and they work tirelessly to heal the planet. We can partner with these angels to give extra power to this work.

Virtue angels also work to create harmony between nations, and we can greatly assist them in this very important work. There are many situations in the world at present that need the wisdom and harmonizing power of angels to bring peace where there is conflict.

SECOND HIERARCHY, SIXTH CHOIR

Powers Angels

Powers angels are very powerful, and it is a joy to work with them, for they are the angels who combat evil in our world. Whether or not you believe in evil, the work of the Powers angels is to bring forth the love and goodness of the human heart and to wipe out negativity, or "evil," in all its forms. Every day we hear news of various instances of so-called evil in the world, from drug dealing to child abuse. The work of the Powers angels to combat this negative attitude of the human heart is very powerful indeed, and our work in assisting them in carrying out their work cannot be underestimated. Someone, somewhere, will be touched by angel wings, and a little bit more of the positive power of the human heart will be awakened somewhere in the world.

Third Hierarchy, Seventh Choir

Principality Angels

Principality angels work to protect endangered species and give their help to all who work for that cause.

Principalities also assist organizations that campaign for human rights and those that work to eradicate discrimination in all its forms. If you feel discriminated against for some reason, these are the angels to work with. Principalities bring their power to bear where there is injustice in the world, particularly where discrimination is an issue, such as when tensions exist between differing faiths or different races or tribes. Work done with the Principality angels is very effective in bringing harmony to bear when such tensions arise.

Principalities are also the angels who are guardians of towns and cities. There are positive and negative aspects of a city, and we can work with the angels to concentrate on the positive energies that are inherent in urban areas. There are many different angels working in a city, including various creative angels and the nature angels who watch over parks and wildlife.

THIRD HIERARCHY, EIGHTH CHOIR

Archangels

Archangels are perhaps the best known of all the angels, for they are the angels who have most often appeared to humankind with messages from God. There are said to be seven archangels, each with different attributes.

ARCHANGEL MICHAEL

Michael was the first angel created by God, and his name means "who is like God." He protects the weak from injustice, and to share in this work can be very satisfying indeed. Sending Michael's love and protection into the world will bring a renewed positive energy to your soul.

ARCHANGEL RAPHAEL

Raphael's name means "healing power of God." He is a very powerful healer and is also concerned with altruistic love. Meditation with Raphael will bring the healing power of God to your body and help dismiss the fear that serious illness can bring, bringing to your heart a new confidence in your recovery.

ARCHANGEL URIEL

Uriel's name means "God is my light." This archangel is considered to be one of the wisest angels because of his wide-ranging knowledge. If you need inspiration in your life, this is the angel to call on, for he will bring fresh ideas when they are needed. Perhaps your life has become rather humdrum and you know that a new course of action is needed, but you do not know what to do. Uriel, with his great wisdom, will point you in the right direction and help you turn around your life in the most positive manner. Perhaps you know what you want to achieve in life but don't know the way to go about it. Archangel Uriel will show you the way and bring inspiration to achieve your dreams.

ARCHANGEL GABRIEL

Gabriel's name means "strength of God." He is the messenger of God and will bring you messages if you have asked a question about your spiritual path. Gabriel is also the angel to help if you are going through a major change in life. His assistance will help things run smoothly and give you the courage to cope with the transition.

Archangel Chamuel

Chamuel's name means "he who seeks God." This archangel can provide great assistance to those on the spiritual path. The spiritual quest can be confusing at times, but Chamuel will guide you through it to find the right answers to your questions and bring you to a place of knowing and deep peace.

One of the most confusing issues on the spiritual path is that of wealth and money. Chamuel can help you put this issue into perspective and will help if you have financial problems. It is often the case that those on the spiritual path regard money in a negative light, and then they wonder why they have money problems! Archangel Chamuel will bring you to the understanding that prosperity is the right of every child of God and that money does not have to be a negative influence in the world. There are many instances where the greed for wealth brings a negative attitude, but that does not mean the money itself is evil or that everyone should be poor. Money can be used for positive reasons, and Archangel Chamuel will bring to you the realization that abundance is your birthright.

Archangel Jophiel

Jophiel's name means "beauty of God." This is the angel of art and beauty. If you wish to be more creative in your life, this is the angel to tune in to. Meditation with Jophiel will bring inspiration to your heart and mind, whether you are suffering from a creative block or you wish to explore latent creative talents.

Archangel Jophiel will also bring his great love to heal your soul if you feel depressed or down about something. Regular meditation with Jophiel will lift your spirits and bring joy to your heart once again.

Archangel Raguel

Raguel's name means "friend of God," and he is an angel of justice and fairness. He will also bring confidence to those who lack it. Meditation with Raguel will bring a newfound confidence to your heart—the kind of confidence that can come only from God.

Third Hierarchy, Ninth Choir

The Angels

Known simply as "angels," this is the choir of angels who work ceaselessly to bring the word of God to the hearts of humankind. That word is love and is the magic ingredient needed to bring healing to one's life at all levels. Angels are intermediaries between humans and God and are often the angels who make themselves visible to human beings. They are the angels involved in "angel sightings." These angels are present at birth and death and any form of transformation, and will protect you if you are in danger. Angels are also nature angels overseeing the development and growth of individual plants. It is from this realm of angels that our Guardian Angels come.

Chapter 7

SERAPHIM ANGELS:
HEALING WHEN DISASTERS STRIKE

Natural disasters make us aware of our oneness with all people on earth. We can feel helpless observing the despair and difficulties faced by the survivors and rescue workers, and while we can donate money to relief efforts, that may feel insufficient. Giving money is a great help on the physical level, but we may want to help heal the grief and trauma suffered by the survivors.

Prayer through meditation with the Seraphim angels, who watch over humanity at such times, is a very powerful way to constructively help all involved in such disasters. The Seraphim are also the angels to tune in to when there has been a terrorist attack in which many people were injured or died.

Wherever there is human suffering on a large scale, the Seraphim angels are there to bring their love and healing. Over recent years, there seems to have been a large increase in the number of terrorist attacks and natural disasters, such as flooding, tsunamis, and earthquakes. So when either a natural or a humanmade disaster happens, endangering the lives of hundreds or thousands of people, you can tune in to the Seraphim, who are pure love, and see the light from them enfolding the whole disaster area. You won't feel so helpless and will feel that you are actually doing something physical to help.

The Seraphim will bring encouragement to the hearts of all those involved with rescue and aid work, and they will also bring their great love to those who survive and feel the grief of having lost loved ones. Seraphim angels can help heal the trauma of living through such disasters, and if this is done through the dedicated medium of someone on the earth plane, their work is so much more powerful.

Working with angels in this way brings powerful healing on the spiritual level to every human being involved in the disaster and can fill the void of helplessness that we feel due to the overwhelming despair of such events.

It is worth remembering that each individual involved in a disaster has a Guardian Angel to help, but when a person is involved in such events, it is difficult to keep contact with the spiritual reality of his or her being. This is where the powerful love of the Seraphim can help so much by breaking through the shock and grief and bringing comfort, hope, and upliftment to the despairing.

By practicing this work with the Seraphim angels, you will be contacting the divine heart of your soul, which will bring a deep satisfaction and love that will flood your whole being. It is this divine love that you need to send into the world to heal and uplift all those caught up in the darkest of hours. This love will also penetrate your own life, and you will feel more at peace as you go about your daily tasks. Working from the divine love at the center of your being will bring its own rewards.

The Seraphim angels sing a beautiful song: "Glory, glory, glory, the earth is full of His glory." This means that everyone on earth, all living creatures, are glorious creatures of great power and beauty. This is the truth about ourselves. We are beings of great power, and however small you think your contribution may be to the healing of humankind, you are in fact making a big, positive difference. Never forget the song of the Seraphim as you go about your work with the angels to bring healing not only to yourself but to all humanity and the planet.

Prayer to the Seraphim

Dearest Seraphim angels, bring your light to the darkness that strikes humankind and shine this wondrous light on their fears and despair. We thank you for your love that brings upliftment in the darkest of hours and pray that our own light within can contribute to the healing work.

Meditation with the Seraphim for Healing

Prepare yourself for meditation by sitting before your angel altar and concentrating on your natural breathing rhythm. Light your candle and remember that the flame represents the light of God that shines in every soul on earth. Make sure your back is straight and your feet are firmly on the floor, if sitting on a chair. You may feel more at ease by crossing your feet. Say the prayer to the Seraphim angels to focus your mind on the work you are about to undertake. Close your eyes and do the relaxation exercise detailed in chapter 2, then imagine yourself in your own special temple. Your Guardian Angel welcomes you joyously and enfolds you in a loving golden light.

Bring to mind the name of the area you wish to help. Say it quietly to yourself or visualize a scene of it and concentrate on your intention to work with the angels. Imagine a beautiful angel standing before you dressed in violet, for this is the color of the Seraphim, the color of healing power. Feel at one with the angel in his or her love for all humanity. See a beautiful violet light surrounding the angel and filling the whole of your temple. Say again quietly to yourself the name of the disaster area, and see the light of the angel shining over the whole area.

Besides the Guardian Angel of each individual involved in the disaster, there are also the angels of the particular region. This is a lot of angel power that can be called upon to assist the Seraphim in their work. Imagine the whole area awash with the light of angels, a beautiful yet powerful light. If you wish, imagine the light to be violet in color, the color of the Seraphim.

Try to put aside any emotional feelings you have regarding the disaster, such as sadness or horror at the scale of it, or hate and anger at the perpetrators of such a crime, for this will make the angels' work more difficult. Try to remain detached, and imagine with sharp clarity the light of angels surrounding the whole scene. Know that this light will assist the survivors and rescue workers alike.

Concentrate on this image for as long as you feel comfortable, and then bring your attention back to your breathing. Give thanks that you are able to assist the Seraphim angels in their work for humankind in this way, and also send the angels your love. You can do this by saying the words "My love to you, dear angels" quietly to yourself, or send a ray of rose light from your heart center to the angel concerned, whichever you feel most at ease with. Close down your chakras as detailed in chapter 2.

This meditation can be performed for any natural disaster, such as an earthquake, a tsunami, a rail or plane disaster, or any act of terrorism. If possible, repeat this meditation daily until you feel your work is done in the matter. Do not doubt your ability to help the angels in this work, for the angels bring the truth to us that we are very powerful beings, and our work with angels in this way always brings comfort and support. Your work with angels and the light will bring hope to the hearts of many and courage to start anew and rebuild shattered lives with a positive heart.

Chapter 8

CHERUBIM ANGELS:
PROTECTION FROM NEGATIVITY

Cherubim are angels of harmony and wisdom, and they provide protection from negative sources, so if you feel you need protecting in some way, these are the angels to call upon. If you find yourself in a negative or threatening situation and want some protection, call on the Cherubim angels and imagine a beautiful angel with his or her wings wrapped around you in the most comforting manner. It will be the Cherubim who will come at such times and bring positive energy to bear on the situation.

A friend of mine named Caroline found herself in one such situation at work. She was attending a meeting and it became obvious that one member of the team had a very negative attitude toward her and took pleasure in pointing out her mistakes in a way that made her look foolish and inadequate for the job. Despite her distress and despair at how to handle the situation, she kept calm and imagined a Cherubim angel enfolding her in love and protection. She really felt the comforting aura of the angel enveloping her, and her mind became clearer to the responses she needed to give. She was able to handle the situation in a positive manner and was able to reply to the various criticisms of her work in a way that proved herself more than adequate for the job. No harm was done to Caroline's work prospects.

This example proves how willing angels are to come to our aid if we make the effort to contact them and ask for help. No matter how small the problem may seem to be, the angels are always ready to give their love and support, for no task is ever too insignificant for them if it causes someone distress. They understand the vulnerability of the ego and are always willing to protect and uplift us and bring positive energy to any situation.

If you are feeling threatened in any way, the following meditation will bring the Cherubim to your side to protect and heal the situation.

Prayer to the Cherubim

Dearest Cherubim angels, I give thanks for your protection at this time in my life, and know that I am safe and well cared for with your love and guidance. Your positive energy fills my heart, and I know that with your help I can deal with all difficult situations.

Meditation with the Cherubim for Protection

Sit before your altar and light your candle, remembering that the flame represents the power of the Divine that is within you. Your Guardian Angel is with you as always to offer added protection and support. Say the prayer to the Cherubim and then relax.

Visualize yourself in your special temple, and see before you the beautiful light of the Cherubim angel. The light from the angel enfolds you in a wonderfully protecting aura. This light permeates your whole being, bringing wisdom to enable you to deal with the situation in the most positive way. Ideas will come to you on how to resolve the situation, and you will know that there is nothing to fear, for angels are by your side every moment of every day radiating protective energy that enfolds you.

Visualize the other person(s) in a golden light as well, as this will greatly heal the situation. As an added protective measure, visualize yourself in the center of a cross of light in a circle of light. Hold this vision and feeling for as long as comfortable, then bring your awareness back to your surroundings. Close down your chakras as detailed in chapter 2, then take a sip of water to further ground yourself. Give thanks to the Cherubim for their help and protection. The next time you feel threatened, just hold yourself in the loving wings of the Cherubim angel and you will immediately feel safe and able to cope with the situation.

If there is some kind of immediate threat, hold yourself in a cross of light in a circle of light together with the enfolding wings of the Cherubim angel, and this will give you immediate protection.

Chapter 9

CHERUBIM ANGELS:
ACCESSING POSITIVE ENERGY
AND FINDING BALANCE

We all feel that we could benefit from some positive energy at certain times in our lives, but how to get it is quite a problem when we are feeling overworked, stressed out, or run-down physically. When we feel like this, it is easy to adopt a negative outlook on life, and even the smallest of problems can seem overwhelming. This, in turn, makes us feel unable to cope, which brings more negativity to our thinking and feeling, and so a vicious circle of negative energy is created that is very difficult to break out of.

The Cherubim angels understand how easy it is to fall into a trap of negativity, and they have the ability to cut through this vicious circle and restore well-being and harmony to your life. They are angels of boundless love and are capable of bringing a renewed energy to your mind and body. A simple meditation with the Cherubim angels is a safe and productive way to bring enthusiasm and excitement back into your life, which will in turn create a positive outlook and bring fresh energy and a renewed vitality.

This positive energy of the Divine is the energy that vitalizes the whole universe and creates all things that are good and constructive. This same power that keeps the planets moving and the seasons turning flows through us and comes directly from the Divine. The Cherubim can help us access this divine energy for our positive good when we feel cut off from it and depleted in some way.

The Cherubim angels will help replace feelings of fatigue and an inability to cope with a new sense of enthusiasm and joy. Their gentle wisdom will give you insights into how you can slow down and sort out your priorities, thereby bringing about a more balanced lifestyle. A healthy balance between work and leisure is essential to harmonious living, and the meditation with the Cherubim in this chapter will help restore this balance by bringing you the wisdom to sort out and rebalance your life. This will give you a positive outlook on life, which will energize your whole being, and so a circle of positive energy is created instead of a negative one.

It may be that you are not overworked or stressed but quite the opposite, and are just in a lethargic and negative state of mind and physical being that makes you give up and feel "What's the use?" toward many things that once gave you pleasure. It is very difficult to break out of this state of mind, for negativity feeds on negative thought patterns, just as positivity feeds on positive thought patterns. Lethargy comes all too easily with a negative outlook on life, but the positive energy of the Cherubim angels can break through this damaging cycle of negative thoughts and bring motivation and joy back to your heart and mind.

This is the special magic of the Cherubim: the ability to break the vicious cycle of negativity and heal the mind and body of their lackluster state. The Cherubim bring the power and warmth of the sun to our lives to transmute lethargy and negative feelings into joyous energy and enthusiasm for life. The Cherubim reconnect us to our inner selves, where the boundless energy of the spirit lies, that energy which is of God and which is our birthright.

With the help of the Cherubim, we feel once again the positive energy that brings fresh determination to take on life's challenges and the inspiration to live our lives to the full.

Feelings of lethargy may also come to us if we are run-down after an illness. The gentle golden light of the Cherubim will bring about a marvelous healing. It will feel as though the summer sun is gently flooding the body and soul, bringing about a wonderful healing and renewed energy. I have often used this meditation when I have been run-down after a viral infection or cold. It is a remarkable pick-me-up and puts some zing back into my life!

The following meditation with the Cherubim will revitalize your mind and body and bring insights on how to live your life in a more balanced and joyful manner.

Prayer to the Cherubim

Dearest Cherubim angels, we give thanks for your positive energy that warms our hearts and brings a refreshed energy back to our tired souls. Remind us of the light that shines within us that is of God, and help us realize the potential of our spirit. Show us the way to use our energy wisely, for our good and for the good of others.

Meditation with the Cherubim for Positive Energy

Sit comfortably with a straight back before your altar, and take a few deep breaths to relax yourself. If you wish, light your candle and remind yourself that the flame represents the light and energy within that is part of the Divine. Say the prayer to the Cherubim angels to focus your mind, and prepare yourself with the relaxation technique detailed in chapter 2.

Imagine the temple you have created for yourself, and feel yourself sitting in it before its simple altar. Your Guardian Angel is with you to offer support. Before you stands a beautiful angel radiating a golden light that enfolds you and makes you feel very safe and warm. This golden light permeates your whole being—mind, body, and soul—and brings a refreshing energy to your heart and mind. Feel this golden light revitalizing every cell of your body, bringing positivity and inspiration to heal your life of negative tendencies, disharmony, and lethargy.

If overwork is your problem, know that the golden light of the Cherubim brings wisdom to your mind and soul to help heal disharmony and bring about a more balanced way of living. You know that you have the energy to cope with all of life's ups and downs.

If lethargy and fatigue are your problem, feel the golden light of the Cherubim angel stimulating every cell of your being, transforming your negative state into one of renewed positive energy.

This powerful golden light brings back motivation and enthusiasm to your soul and gives you insight into how you can make your life happier and more interesting. Lethargy and its negative outlook dissolve away in this golden light, and you know that this is the start of a more joyful way of living.

Bathe yourself in this golden light for as long as you feel comfortable, then bring your awareness back to your breathing. Become aware of your actual surroundings, and close your chakras as detailed in chapter 2. Take a few sips of water to ground yourself further, and don't forget to put out your candle!

Give thanks to the Cherubim angel for his or her positive help, which will bring so much healing to your life. Make a note of any insights that came to you during the meditation, and also be alert over the next day or so for any ideas that come to you about leading a more positive and joyous life.

Chapter 10

THRONE ANGELS:
HEALING RELATIONSHIP ISSUES AND LONELINESS

Relationships define our lives and can determine whether we are happy or sad, angry or content. When things are going well in our relationships, life can feel pretty good, but when there is disharmony between ourselves and someone close to us, this can affect our well-being to a serious degree. The distress caused can affect all areas of our lives.

Throne angels understand how disharmony in a relationship can arise. Usually it is because one person feels threatened in some way. When our views or opinions are challenged, we can feel under threat, and when we feel undermined or criticized, feelings of being diminished can arise, which can be quite scary for the ego.

Thrones understand these dilemmas and are in no way judgmental. It is important to understand that no angel is ever in any way judgmental toward you. Their only wish is to bring love and healing to difficult situations. Thrones understand relationship issues in particular and will bring their love and healing to your life. You only need to ask, and meditation is one of the surest ways to get this help. Throne angels will show you the best way to proceed to heal the relationship and bring harmony and happiness back to your life.

All relationships are mirrors held up to ourselves. How we think about ourselves will affect the types of relationships we attract. We often look to other people to bring us fulfillment and approval, to bring that which is missing from our lives, whereas it is only ourselves who can bring fulfillment and meaning to our lives. Thrones understand and can help us highlight the problems within that may be causing a negative effect to blight our relationships.

When we have difficulties with someone, it is no use trying to change them or make them see our point of view. The only person we can change is ourselves, and with the help of angels we can restore harmony to a friendship or relationship.

It is not always easy to forgive when we have been hurt in some way, but the Throne angels can open a channel to allow healing to take place. When we are hurt, forgiveness suggests weakness, and the desire to be strong in the situation suggests retaliation in some way. But real strength of character comes with forgiveness and healing, and even if this seems impossible, the Throne angels can help by bringing their own healing balm to our hearts and showing us the way to proceed to heal the situation.

Non-forgiveness leaves us in the other person's power, for non-forgiveness means we are holding on to the situation and not letting go of the hurt that it brings. Why spend our time in someone else's power? We need to take back our power and heal the situation. There is no weakness in forgiveness. Throne angels understand how hard forgiveness can be, especially when we have been deeply hurt, but their healing power will bring a new resolve to our souls and healing to our hearts.

It is important to remember that we cannot change anyone to fit our point of view; we can only change our reaction to the situation. This is why meditation with the Throne angels is so helpful, for they can bring the love and wisdom of

God to our hearts and minds, thereby enabling us to see the situation in a clearer light and realize the action that needs to be taken.

It may be that it is time to move on from a relationship, in which case the Throne angels will give you all their love and support. Thrones understand the pain this may cause and will bring their healing to your heart. If the person you are at odds with is a relative, friend, or partner you don't wish to break with, Thrones will bring their wisdom and healing to the situation.

Thrones can shine the light of love on the situation, illuminating possibilities for healing and reconciliation. They will bring ideas to your mind that can help you reach a compromise or let go of the problem altogether. You will know that the idea comes from the angels, for it will give you a good feeling in your solar plexus, and you will know in your heart of hearts that it is a positive way to move forward. You will feel comfortable with the idea, even though you are free to disregard any ideas the angels give you, for angels cannot force you to do anything.

If loneliness is your problem, meditation with the Throne angels is a wonderful way to attract the right sort of people into your life. Thrones will give you inspiration and ideas on how to meet like-minded people. Indeed, just working with the various angels in this book will bring a purpose to your life and also attract new friendships, for you will be radiating a positive energy that will attract positive things into your life and bring a wonderful healing to areas of your life that you wish to improve.

To work on your relationships and bring harmony and joy to them, the following simple meditation is all that is necessary.

PRAYER TO THE THRONES

Beloved Throne angels, open our hearts to the pleasures of friendship and companionship and bless the friendships and relationships that we have. We pray that you will bring your beautiful healing where there is disharmony or loneliness and also bring your healing and love where there is closure.

MEDITATION WITH THE THRONES TO HEAL RELATIONSHIP ISSUES AND LONELINESS

Sit before your angel altar in a chair or on the floor, and say the prayer to the Throne angels either out loud or quietly to yourself. Light your candle to remind yourself of the light of God that shines within every heart. Make yourself comfortable and close your eyes. Concentrate on your breathing, and let the steady, natural rhythm of your breath help still your mind and prepare you for meditation. Perform the relaxation exercise detailed in chapter 2, and then imagine yourself in your inner temple, that sacred space within where you are safe and secure. Your Guardian Angel stands beside you to give you support.

Concentrate on your temple for a few moments to really still and calm the mind, and then imagine a beautiful angel standing in front of you. There is light emanating from the angel of a lovely rose color, the color of love and friendship. Feel a ray of this light concentrating on your heart center and filling you with a warm glow of love for yourself and all humankind. Absorb this rose-colored light into every cell of your being and radiate it out into the world as a positive power for good. Know that by sending love and light out into the world, you are not only sending a healing power into the world, but are also attracting positive relationships into your life. The angel gives you all of his or her love. Feel it filling you, and give thanks to the angel for the love and support. Hold this feeling of absorbing and radiating love for as long as you feel comfortable, and know that all is well in your life.

If you have a particular problem with someone that you wish to work on, perform the following exercise. Otherwise, bring your awareness back to your breath and your actual surroundings. Give thanks once again to the angel for his or her love, then close down your chakras as detailed in chapter 2.

For help in resolving a problem with someone by bringing forgiveness to your heart, imagine that the Throne angel creates a large figure eight made out of rose-colored light. You are seated in one section and the person you wish to resolve matters with is seated in the other half. The angel stands at the intersection with arms stretched out to each side, bathing you both in light. It may help to say something like, "I would really like help in resolving issues with…." This will focus the mind and also act as an affirmation to yourself that you really want to heal this situation.

Feel the warmth and love of the angel light, and know that its healing magic is working to resolve issues between you both. Ideas may come to you on how you could heal the situation, so be ready to jot them down after the meditation. Don't worry if no ideas come. The healing magic will continue to work on you both for some time, so be prepared for some surprises over the next few days. Hold the feeling of the two of you being held in the light and love of the angel for as long as is comfortable, then see the other person dissolve away together with the figure eight. The angel remains to flood you with light, which you feel in every cell of your being.

Gradually bring your awareness back to your breathing and to your actual surroundings. Thank the Throne angel for his or her help in the matter, and give the angel your love. Close down your chakras as detailed in chapter 2.

Over the next few days, be aware of any feelings or ideas you have about the situation and be prepared to act on them. Your Guardian Angel will give you the courage needed to act on any ideas that come to you. You will be surprised at how quickly and gently angel healing works!

Chapter 11

DOMINION ANGELS:
ACCESSING INNER WISDOM

Inner wisdom is something we all seek at some time in our lives, especially when we have made mistakes. We often find ourselves in a position where a little wisdom would help to sort out some problem, but our ego can lead us along a negative path that goes nowhere. Perhaps you have come to a point in your life where you realize there is more to you than just the everyday ego personality and you wish to find the divine spark within that will give you the wisdom to realize your true potential in life.

Dominions are angels of intuition and wisdom and are the angels to contact if you want to work on your inner wisdom. They also have in their care all religious organizations on earth, and they bring their divine wisdom to church leaders and also to political leaders. If you find yourself in a situation where you need some divine wisdom to help you sort things out, call upon the Dominion angels in meditation to bring you the guidance you need. Likewise, if there is a situation in the world that needs divine wisdom, meditate with the Dominion angels and help them bring their guidance to the situation.

Dominion angels remind us that we are spiritual beings and the sole purpose of our lives on earth is to grow spiritually and find our true selves. Our true selves reveal altruistic love for all humankind, which we can send out into the world for the good of all. Finding our true spiritual selves can bring us the greatest joy and peace, for we know that all is well in our lives and life's problems melt away or become easier to deal with when seen in the light of the spirit. Our true inner selves bring us divine wisdom with which we can work miracles in our lives.

The layers of material life grow thick and prevent us from seeing our true inner nature, but the meditations in this book will open us up to that true self. Remember the song of the Seraphim, "the earth is full of His glory," and remember that we are truly glorious beings capable of great things and partners to the angels in their tireless work for humankind and all living creatures on the earth.

Our true spiritual self is not something we "put on" just for one day a week or when we meditate; it is not something different from our everyday self. Realizing our true inner self is living our everyday life to the best of our ability and appreciating the abundance and magnificence of our world. It is relating to people in the kindest and most thoughtful way, be they friends, work colleagues, or strangers, however much they might annoy us, and being as kind and understanding as we possibly can. Finding our true spiritual self won't turn us into saints, but our spiritual self can give us the understanding and patience to put annoying and irritating matters into perspective and bring us to a place of peace. That sums up our spiritual self: it is always acting and reacting from a place of joy and peace within, no matter how irritating or hurtful someone is being or however tedious the task at hand is.

When we come up against a problem or a brick wall in our plans, our spiritual self can lead us to that inner wisdom within that can shine the light of the spirit on problems and help sort them out. Dominion angels can help us find our "still, small voice within" that whispers to us of the joy and magnificence of our true selves. It is a voice that speaks to us of how false our fears and worries are that torment us so. Dominion angels remind us that we are truly glorious beings.

Dominion angels can give us the courage to act when action is needed and also give us the wisdom and insight to act creatively and thoughtfully. By connecting us to that inner spiritual self, Dominion angels can help us live a harmonious life by not overreacting to the trials and tribulations that everyday life brings. They tell us that all is well in our lives and fears and worries are groundless. By bringing us to that place of peace within, Dominion angels help us realize that all is as it should be and all is working out according to a divine plan for our lives. Dominions bring us a message of joy and point out that the wisdom of our spiritual self can direct us safely through any problems we have.

Only our spiritual self can bring us the peace and joy we search for in life through material possessions. Material acquisitions may bring us a limited degree of peace and joy, but there is always something that comes along to upset the equilibrium of life. The deep peace we find through connecting to our spiritual self is always there for us and will never let us down. It will bring us the wisdom needed to deal with life's upsets, and joy will always be in our hearts when we connect to that spark of the Divine within. Dominion angels connect us to the truth of our real self that knows the divine and eternal peace and joy of our spirit. Our divine spirit will bring to our hearts that which is everlasting and positive. It is complete in itself, unlike the materialistic, which cannot satisfy our true needs.

Dominion angels help us achieve this deep, everlasting peace that can steer our lives through untroubled waters and make every day a joyful adventure.

Dominion angels can give us the help we need to still the mind of its worries that go round and round, causing unnecessary turmoil in our hearts. By revealing to us the magic of our spiritual selves, Dominion angels help us take control of our thoughts, and thereby our lives, and the peace within shows us the way to keep our thoughts positive and healthy. When we have a difficult situation to deal with, it is very difficult to keep our thoughts about it positive. All sorts of feelings can make our thoughts negative and unhealthy. But by actively seeking the wisdom of the still, small voice within, with the help of the Dominion angels, positive thoughts can take control, and it is amazing how problems can dissolve away or seem small when the light of the spirit is shone on them. By uniting with the divine self within, difficult karma can be dissolved and we can find that our life is much happier and trouble-free.

Meditation with the Dominion angels will give us the ability to access our spiritual self at will, and regular practice of the meditation in this chapter will bring the peace and joy of the inner self to our hearts for longer and longer periods.

Our spiritual self is not something remote that is only accessible by meditation. Our spiritual self is as naturally a part of us as our eyes and ears are, but it is hidden under layers of the ego. The meditation with the Dominion angels will melt these layers away, revealing to us the true beauty and power of our real selves. This power is a true and positive power that can work miracles in our lives, and Dominion angels can help us access it.

This power is far greater than any power of the ego, or the earth self, and it is the divine purpose of the Dominion angels to help humankind find and use this positive power for the good of the individual and the good of all humankind. When we access this divine power through our inner spiritual self, we not only feel a great love for ourselves that brings an understanding of our so-called faults, but we also feel at peace with ourselves. This spiritual peace brings a strength and wisdom that can help us overcome the problems of life and make us realize that we *are* good enough.

The following meditation will bring the Dominion angels to your side to assist you in accessing the wonderful love, wisdom, and peace of your inner spirit.

Prayer to the Dominions

Beloved Dominion angels, bring your sweet presence to our lives and reveal to us the true loving nature of our spiritual selves. Reveal to us the deep peace and wisdom that is ours to work with for good in our lives and for the good of humankind, and help us have confidence in the inner light that is of divine power.

Meditation with the Dominions to Find Divine Wisdom Within

Sit comfortably either in a chair or on the floor in front of your altar, and breathe deeply for a few moments to clear your mind. Light your candle as a reminder of the little light that glows within you as a part of the Divine. Say the prayer to the Dominion angels to focus your mind and relax your body, particularly your shoulders, as detailed in chapter 2. Imagine yourself in your own special temple. You feel very safe and happy in your temple, with your Guardian Angel beside you to give help and support.

Before you stands a beautiful angel surrounded by a soft white light tinged with rose and yellow, the colors of love and wisdom. Feel this light filling every cell of your being and opening your heart center to the love of the Divine. You feel a great love flooding through you and illuminating your whole being. Feel your aura being filled with the beautiful light from the Dominion angel. A great peace fills your heart and mind, and you feel more relaxed and happy and at peace with the world than you have been in a long time. Bathe yourself in this light and enjoy the peace and love that fill your heart. Relax into this light for as long as you feel comfortable. Know that all is well in your life and that life's problems can be transformed into positive endeavors when viewed from the peace of the spirit.

If you have a particular problem and feel in need of some divine wisdom to help you through it, gently focus on it without getting emotionally involved and feel the light of the Dominion angels flooding your whole being. Answers and inspiration will come to you, if not immediately, then in the next day or so.

When you feel ready, imagine the light from your heart center mingling with the light from the angel, and see this light filling your whole temple and the surrounding area.

Then imagine this light going out into the world to bring wisdom and love where they are needed most. This angel light will heal the hearts and minds of all humankind and bring peace and love where there is distress and disharmony for whatever reasons. Enjoy working with the angels in this way to bring peace and love to humankind. Send this light into the world for as long as you feel able, then slowly bring your attention back to your actual surroundings. Take a few deep breaths to bring yourself fully back, and close down your chakras as detailed in chapter 2. Take a sip of water, if necessary, to fully ground yourself. Remember to snuff out your candle if you lit one!

Thank the Dominion angel for his or her love and wisdom that has penetrated your heart, and also for radiating this love and wisdom to all of humankind.

Connecting with the spark of the Divine within will bring great spiritual rewards to you, for the greatest peace will flow through you and will bring harmony to your life where there is disharmony and peace where there is turmoil. The more you practice this meditation, the more you will feel in tune with your spiritual self and feel guided and protected by a great strength and love. I found that I experienced a very warm and happy feeling in my heart center when I began practicing this meditation, and I found I had more wisdom to deal with difficult situations in my life. Sending the light of the angel into the world also brings a wonderful feeling of fulfillment, for it is the work our spirits yearn for.

Chapter 12

VIRTUE ANGELS:
HELPING WITH GREEN ISSUES

Virtue angels are very much concerned with looking after the earth in all its aspects, from the deepest of the oceans to the tiniest wildflower. Their care for the planet is limitless and all-encompassing. The awareness of green issues that has grown over the past years may be because we are more in touch with angels and they have been able to bring their care of the planet to human attention. As awareness of angels over the past hundred years or so has grown, so have our minds been opened to the needs of the earth and all that grows and lives upon it. Most of us today would say that we are aware of green issues and that we do our bit to help heal and safeguard the planet, be it only recycling.

Virtue angels bring the light of wisdom to those in positions of power in the world to heighten their awareness of green issues. They have the whole earth very much in their care, and they work tirelessly to heal the planet. We can partner with the angels in this respect to give extra power to their work.

If you lead a busy life with little free time, it is easy to think that other people can give their time more easily, particularly those who carry out much-needed conservation work. But if you are unable to give any time in such a way, it only takes five or ten minutes to make contact with the Virtue angels and send their healing into the world. It will make their work so much more powerful, and the work will not be wasted in any way whatsoever.

The angels do not apportion any blame for things that go wrong in the world, and in no way do they stand in judgment of us. They accept and are pleased that human beings are now taking positive action to rectify much of the damage done to the earth by human progress in all its guises.

So, if angels are working ceaselessly to heal the planet, how and why do accidents like oil spills happen, causing devastation to local environments and suffering to wild-life? We should remember that humans have free will—that is, free will to use oil in their everyday lives, free will to drill for oil and to transport it, and so forth. Accidents happen, but the love of angels is not diminished in any way when there is such an occurrence. Indeed, angels work tirelessly to help humans clean up the mess. Part of their work is to stimulate the hearts and minds of human beings to restore harmony and balance to the earth.

Virtue angels work very closely with the ninth choir of angels, the angels that look after all wildlife and individual plants. Their love is for every living creature and plant that inhabits the earth. Many nature spirits, or faeries, help the angels in this work.

Here is a beautiful example of how angels look after all the plants and trees on the planet. It was related to me by my friend Doreen, who is a firm believer in angels and also works with them on a regular basis.

Doreen's back garden adjoined land that was to be re-developed. A hazel tree that overhung her garden needed to be cut down to make way for the new development. She was very fond of this tree and was very sad that it needed to be cut down. On the day prior to the work being carried out, Doreen spoke to the angel of the tree and warned him of the impending work, and held the tree in healing angel light.

On the evening after the tree had been cut down, Doreen had the most beautiful vision. She saw the angel of the tree standing where the tree had been, holding a large staff. He knocked it on the ground a couple of times, and fairies appeared from the undergrowth and twirled around the staff. The tree angel seemed to use his staff to "scoop up" the fairies and tree spirits that had belonged to the tree. They fluttered and twirled around the staff like little lights, and then the tree angel walked off into the distance with his little out-of-work and homeless band, maybe to find them a new home and another tree to look after.

Before he left, the angel of the tree acknowledged Doreen's presence by giving a slight nod of his head. Maybe that was a thank you for Doreen's care and love for the tree.

This demonstrates how every living plant and creature, including humans, are looked after by angels every minute of every day. The angels' love and support are there waiting for us to tap in to, a love and support that will make such a difference in the everyday trials and tribulations of our lives. Working with the Virtue angels to heal the world will especially bring a sense of contentment and wonderment and bring insights into how the angels go about their work. You may even be fortunate enough to have a vision like Doreen's.

I had a wonderful vision of a Virtue angel when on a hilltop in Dorset. The hill was quite high and afforded great views of the surrounding countryside. There was no one else around, and as soon as I reached the top of the hill, I became very aware of an angel's presence. I don't think I have ever felt so attuned to angels as I did that day. The angel I "saw" was of immense size, a beautiful creature of white light, and this light covered the whole hilltop and much of the surrounding countryside. I felt a great love in my heart not only for the angel but for everyone on earth. My feeling of love for all living things was immeasurable. I wanted the vision to last forever, for I felt as light as a feather and felt that I, too, was soaring above the hill swathed in the lovely white light of the angel.

The vision gradually receded, but I was left with a wonderful feeling in my heart center that I can recall to this day. My awareness of the beauty of nature was also much sharper than before, and I marveled at each wildflower and plant as though I was seeing them for the first time. The sky, the grass, the trees, and the flowers all resonated with an exquisite beauty and made me feel a wonderful love for all creation. I wanted the feeling to last forever, but it gradually faded and I felt a peace within myself that I had not known for a long time. When I feel a bit depressed or down, I can recall this wonderful feeling and draw it up from my heart center to fill my entire being. I can appreciate the beauty around me regardless of where I am, be it in my garden or walking along a crowded street.

The Virtue angels don't just work in the countryside; they work on all levels and will give their love and support to your own garden if you have one. To bring angel power to your garden, hold each plant in angel light and remember the little fairies and spirits of the plant who are looking after it and know that the angels are watching over them. Send them your love and give thanks to them for the work they do, and feel their love flowing back to you. This will turn your garden into a wonderful place of peace and tranquility, full of angel power, where you can revitalize yourself during the busy days. Working with these nature angels brings its own kind of satisfaction, especially if you work on the land, for this will make your work flow effortlessly and bring you a great sense of achievement.

Even if you don't have a garden of your own, you can still tune in to the Virtue angels and their faerie helpers. If there is a park nearby, practice sending your light to all the trees, shrubs, and plants, and you will experience a great upliftment of your spirit. You can help maintain the area as a haven of peace and tranquility for all who use it, and this will give your soul a wonderful feeling of joy, for you will be working from the divine spark within. The park will flourish as a restorative place for all who go there. Nature has a very restorative effect on our busy lives, and tuning in to nature in this way will bring peace and healing to your soul.

Remember, too, the wildlife in your garden and in the park, and hold them in the beautiful light of the angels. Enjoy the birdsong and know that the angels are working to make a haven for wildlife, which will intensify the joy of using such areas.

Virtue angels send power to all organizations that work for the good of the planet, from worldwide organizations to local nature conservation groups. So if you do not have any time to give but want to help in their work, spend ten minutes a day doing the following meditation. By sending these organizations much-needed support and power with the angels, you will be doing far more than you can possibly imagine. Alternatively, you can practice the meditation once a week if you are short on time, and it will still have the same effect.

Prayer to the Virtues

Dearest Virtue angels, open our hearts and minds to the needs of the earth. We thank you for the work you do to restore harmony and healing to our world. We pray that our work with you will bring healing where it is needed most and benefit all those who work to heal the planet.

Meditation with the Virtues for Help with Green Issues

Sit comfortably before your angel altar and prepare yourself for meditation by concentrating on your natural breathing rhythm. Light your candle to remind yourself of the spark of the Divine that shines within you. Make sure your back is straight and your feet are firmly on the floor if sitting on a chair. You may feel more at ease by crossing your feet. Close your eyes and do the relaxation exercise detailed in chapter 2.

When doing this meditation, I always imagine myself on the hilltop where I saw the vision of the Virtue angel, so you may find it appropriate to imagine yourself also sitting on a hilltop surrounded by wildflowers and trees and with a beautiful blue sky above. Imagine the countryside around the hill, and hear the birds singing and crickets and other insects buzzing around you. Alternatively, there may be a special place of your own where you feel very close to nature and at peace with all creation, so visualize yourself there with as much detail as possible.

Say the prayer to the Virtue angels to focus your mind on the work you are about to undertake. Feel the presence of your Guardian Angel, who gives you all the love and support you need in your work for the planet.

Imagine a great angel of sparkling white light before you. This angel holds the well-being of the whole earth in his or her heart. Tune in to that love, and feel yourself filled with a great love for all creation. Just concentrate on this love and the light of the angel, and see this light as beautiful rays radiating out to encompass the whole world. The whole world is held in the healing light of the Virtue angel.

If there is an organization you wish to support, say its name quietly to yourself and know that the angel is holding all workers of that organization in light and power. Perhaps there has been an environmental disaster, such as an oil spill or a forest fire, to which you would like to send healing light. Either say the name of the particular location to yourself or visualize the scene and know that the angel is sending light and love to all those involved in dealing with it. The light of the angel will also bring healing and new growth where there has been destruction. You can continue this meditation every day until you feel the situation is resolved and your work is complete. Otherwise, practicing the meditation once a week on the same day and at the same time will suffice to bring the angel healing to the planet.

When you feel ready, direct your attention back to your actual surroundings and close down your chakras as detailed in chapter 2. Take a few sips of water to really ground yourself, and know that your light and power will continue to work with the angels long after you have finished your meditation. Don't forget to put out your candle!

Chapter 13

VIRTUE ANGELS:
BRINGING PEACE AND HARMONY TO THE WORLD

Disharmony between nations poses the greatest risks to humankind and can cause distress to millions of people. Virtue angels do not stand in judgment of anyone but bring their healing love to bear on world leaders where there is disharmony, war, and conflict on a national or international scale. You can take part in this healing work by bringing the angels' power to the earth level and giving it extra potency.

World leaders are in positions of great power and can attract to themselves the negative forces that are at large in the world. They are very vulnerable in this respect. But Virtue angels can bring positivity and peace to bear where there is disharmony, and this energy is made even more powerful by dedicated workers on the earth plane. This is very worthwhile work, and if you would like to contribute your power to the angels' work, it should only take about five or ten minutes a day in meditation. Ideally you can do this work weekly on the same day each week and at the same time of day, so your mind gets used to doing the work at that time.

The work may seem daunting, and you may think that it is useless, for how can any individual bring about any real changes in the world? But work with the angels is never wasted and angel power is very real. There really are angels working for world peace, and we cannot know how many times a serious situation has been averted through the intervention of angels.

It is true that every individual in the world matters and has the power to change the world, and with the help of angels this is even more so. Every human being has the power of the Divine within them, and this power should not be underestimated. You may think you cannot possibly make a difference in the world, but you cannot know that this is true. Working with angels does make a difference, and someone, somewhere, will be touched by angel wings and feel the peace and wisdom of the angels in their heart. If this power is directed at those in positions of power in the world, the angels can work their magic tenfold. Don't be disheartened if you feel your work is of no use. All work with angels has some effect somewhere and builds on the positivity and love of the Divine that abounds in the world.

This work will put you in touch with your divine nature, the little spark within, and bring a deep peace to your soul. By sending out the harmonious energy of the angels, you will attract harmony into your own life, and you will feel the benefits of this work in more ways than you thought imaginable. Miracles can happen when angels are involved, and by working with angels for peace and harmony, a deep peace will envelop your soul and your life. Never fear that your efforts are useless, for all angel work makes a difference somewhere in the world.

Wherever there is conflict in the world, angel power can be brought to bear upon it. The altruistic love that you send out when working with angels can bring much-needed wisdom and understanding to difficult situations and will have definite results, for no angel work is ever wasted.

Prayer to the Virtues

Dearest Virtue angels, bring your wisdom and peace where there is disharmony in the world. We pray that our own efforts will bring positive good to bear. Where there is darkness, bring your light, and where there is misunderstanding, bring your wisdom.

Meditation with the Virtues for World Harmony

Sit comfortably either in a chair or on the floor, and have your angel altar in front of you. Contemplate your altar for a few moments, and light your candle to remind yourself of the light that lives within you that is the spark of God. Say the prayer to the Virtue angels to focus your mind on the work you are about to do, then do the relaxation exercise detailed in chapter 2.

When you feel ready and focused, imagine yourself in your inner temple with your Guardian Angel, who welcomes you with outstretched arms of love and joy. He or she stands beside you to support you in the work you are about to undertake.

See before you a beautiful angel radiating a brilliant emerald-green light, the color of harmony, and feel yourself filled with this light in every part of your being. Your whole temple is filled with this light. See this light going out into the world to bring harmony and understanding where it is needed. If you wish, think of a particular world situation that needs angel harmony and love at the present time. Otherwise, just see the light flooding the whole earth and know that the angels will direct the power where it is needed most. Keep this image in your mind for as long as you feel comfortable with it, then bring your attention back to your inner temple and then your actual surroundings. Thank the angel for being there and sending this healing light into the world to bring peace and harmony. Give thanks to yourself also for being able to do this vital work with the angels.

Close your chakras as detailed in chapter 2, paying particular attention to this ritual to really ground yourself, and take a few sips of water to help ground yourself further. Know that your work will not be wasted and that the angels will continue their work of bringing harmony and peace to the world.

The more you do this meditation, the more you will attract harmony into your own life. It is not necessary to perform the meditation every day, but it can be done once a week if you wish. The power of angel magic will not be diminished. Indeed, the more focused and empowered you are, the more effective the angel power will be in the world.

Chapter 14

POWERS ANGELS:
COMBATING EVIL IN THE WORLD

Whether or not you believe in evil, the work of the Powers angels is to bring forth the love and goodness that rest deeply in the human heart and to eradicate negativity, or evil, in all its forms. There are many forms of evil in the world where vulnerable people are exploited by those in power. Children in particular are especially vulnerable. If you feel strongly about a particular type of evil you wish to help combat, focusing on this and asking the Powers angels for help will make a big difference. Powers angels are very powerful, and it is a joy to work with them, for they are the angels who combat evil in our world. To undertake such work with the angels will bring you an everlasting peace deep within your soul and will bring great joy to the angels.

Evil can come about due to the desire for power and greed, which often stems from fear of some kind. The ego is afraid, and power can give comfort to a frightened ego. The thirst for power is one of the most common causes of evil in our world.

Never underestimate the work of the angels, for someone, somewhere, will be touched by angel light and a little bit of evil will be eradicated. Always have confidence in the power of angels and in your own work of helping to radiate angel light and healing on the earth plane. Send out the angel light and know that the angels are working for good in the world, and have faith in this work. Know that you can make a difference through your positive thoughts and healing work, and give thanks for the work the angels do in the world.

Powers angels do not stand in judgment of anyone, however negative or evil the person may appear. They work to bring understanding and love to the world. Their task is to heighten awareness of the spark of the Divine within each soul, a spark that can bring true goodness and love to the consciousness of all humankind. This is the tireless work of the Power angels, and helping them bring this work to the earth plane is very valuable work indeed and will bring an everlasting peace to your soul.

Sending angel healing into the world when there seems to be so much evil and negative power may seem futile, but always believe in the work of the angels. It may take time, but angel work will have an effect somewhere in the world. Do the meditation in this chapter to assist the Powers angels in their work of fighting evil and you will find it most rewarding, for it is some of the most important work you can do. Remember, you are a being of great power, and your work with angels does have a great effect in the world.

Perhaps there is a particular cause that is close to your heart. You can help more than you will ever know by sending angel love into the world.

By doing this work, you will be uniting with the divine spark within you, and this divine spark will grow brighter each time you practice this meditation. Indeed, working with the angels on the various meditations in this book will help the divine spark within to grow more and more on a daily basis until the peace and love of the Divine floods your whole being and you find your life taking on a happier and more worthwhile aspect. Sending angel healing into the world will bring a subtle healing to your life, and any negativity and disappointments will gradually melt away and transform into wonderful positive opportunities that bring a happiness and contentment you never thought you could acquire.

The news media do tend to concentrate on all the negative aspects of the world, which can be rather depressing. Someone said to me recently, "I wish we could have some good news for a change." Well, there is good news! Angels walk with us and enfold us in their love every moment of every day and are always there for us when we feel down. They are combating negative conditions and so-called evil in all its forms, and your work with them will make their work so much easier.

Always remember that there is a lot of positive energy in the world that manifests in many ways and combats the evil and injustices that afflict so many. There are many individuals and organizations who work tirelessly to bring comfort and help to both humans and animals who are in some way suffering. Contemplate the goodness that is in the world, and add your own little divine spark to the many divine sparks that light the world. Evil and injustice can be overcome by the goodwill of people everywhere. The angels are with everyone, including those who perpetrate the evil and injustice, and they lift humankind above the negative view of the minority. The angels' love is there for all to experience and is all-powerful.

PRAYER TO THE POWERS ANGELS

Dearest Powers angels, we thank you for your valuable work in fighting evil in the world and know that your work has great effect. Allow us to help you in this most important of work. We pray that our hearts will join with yours in sending healing into the world.

MEDITATION WITH POWERS ANGELS TO COMBAT EVIL IN THE WORLD

Sit in a chair or on the floor, whichever is the most comfortable, and have your angel altar in front of you. Light your candle and concentrate on the flame for a few moments, remembering that this flame represents the spark of God that is deep within the soul of every living being. Say the prayer to the Powers angels, then relax yourself as detailed in chapter 2. Imagine yourself in your own special temple, where your Guardian Angel awaits you. He or she stands behind you with hands on your shoulders to give you support in the work you are about to do.

Imagine in front of you a powerful angel dressed in violet, the color of goodness and power. This angel is full of love and extends his or her arms in welcome to you. You feel very happy that you are able to share in this important work. See the violet rays radiating out from the angel and flooding your temple. Imagine this light spreading out, flooding the whole world in angel light. You may wish to focus on one particular type of evil, in which case just say to yourself a few words that sum it up and don't dwell on the particular issue, for this might distress you. The angel will know exactly what you are thinking and will send his or her love and power appropriately. Otherwise, don't think of any particular thing or person, for the angels know where their help is needed.

Don't dwell on the evil, or negativity, that is in the world, but think instead of all the millions of people in the world who live by the goodness in their hearts and think also of the organizations that work to combat negative conditions. Feel your heart center expanding as you think of them. Send out the light from the angel and the light of your heart center, and feel yourself becoming one with all that is good and positive. See this positive goodness as a glorious light shining over all the earth, and feel yourself become as one with this light. Feel the joy and love it brings to your heart, and know that your work is making a great difference in the world.

Hold this vision for as long as you feel comfortable with it, then let your attention return to your actual surroundings. Know that you have given invaluable help to the Powers angels in their continuous fight against evil in the world. Know that someone, somewhere, will be touched by the light and a difference will be made by your work.

Take a few deep breaths to bring your awareness fully back to the present, and close your chakras to fully ground yourself, as detailed in chapter 2. Take a few sips of water, as this will also help to ground you and bring you fully back from the meditation. You can do this meditation every day if you wish. By doing it at the same time each day, it will focus your mind and you will find it easier to do the work. Alternatively, you can do this meditation once a week on the same day and at the same time, and the work will be just as powerful.

Chapter 15

POWERS ANGELS:
REMOVING NEGATIVE BLOCKS

Powers angels can also help you release negative emotional blocks that are hindering you on the spiritual path. These blocks could go back to childhood, and you could still be suffering from trauma resulting from the incident, but whatever the difficulties are, Powers angels can help unblock the negative energy that is preventing you from moving on and bring you to a place of understanding, love, and forgiveness. Perhaps this block is due to something that was done to you and you find it hard to forgive, or maybe it was something that you did and you cannot forgive yourself. Powers angels are beside you to give you love and uplift you with their understanding. They will gently dissolve the emotional block and help you realize that you did your best at that time.

Incidents from childhood can affect us for the rest of our lives and give us a false sense of who and what we are. If you were victimized as a child, you can remain in a victimized state into adulthood. This will bring negative conditions to your life, for you will not have the confidence to move forward to a state of positive endeavor but instead remain trapped in the false belief that you are no good or that you will never succeed, for you are a loser. Such beliefs are unfounded, for we all have the power of God's light within us to help us overcome all obstacles and live our lives to the very fullest. We can experience the aftereffects of traumatic childhood experiences forever, but the Powers angels can gently heal the hurt and trauma and bring us to a place of forgiveness. Angels are always by our side to give their reassurance, upliftment, and love to help us over the barriers we ourselves put in our way to leading a happy and fulfilling life.

Hanging on to misguided beliefs about yourself can seriously hinder your ability to achieve your goals and dreams in life, for you will not believe that you can really succeed. Such beliefs can have a devastating effect on our lives and prevent us from achieving our true potential.

These beliefs may not be apparent in the personality, for deep-seated negative beliefs about ourselves are exactly that—deep and hidden from our everyday view of ourselves. Such beliefs and feelings lie deep within and cloud our judgment of ourselves, bringing about a misconception of who we are and what we can achieve. Whatever the cause, whether it is something that was done to us or something that we ourselves did and feel ashamed of, the effects in our lives are dramatic.

Powers angels can bring you to a place within where you can let go of negative emotions that are linked to incidents from the past. The angels bring a gentle healing without the need for traumatic soul searching that can be as harmful as the original incident.

Whatever was done to you in the past, the Powers angels can bring gentle healing to your heart and the realization that forgiveness is the only route to take. Whoever it was that hurt you in the past, don't let them ruin your life forever. That is giving them power over you. Why should this person or persons have such power to prevent you from living a happy life? Let go and all will be well, and you will feel a great feeling of release. It helps to physically let go with a great sigh of relief. The meditation in this chapter will greatly assist you in releasing negative emotions from the past.

Hanging on to past hurts and not being able to forgive is something the ego does out of fear. The ego can still feel very threatened by the hurts of long ago, whenever they happened, especially if at the time you felt helpless and vulnerable. No one should be made to feel this way, and the pain that this can bring to the soul can eat into a person and inhibit growth. The ego is still fighting those feelings of helplessness and vulnerability. The ego sees forgiveness as weakness and can feel very threatened by it, but the spirit within is stronger and knows that the person is not vulnerable but has the love and help of the angels at all times. The ego continues to fight the battle long after the actual incident, resulting in despair and nonforgiveness, which cause great distress to the soul. The meditation with the Powers angels in this chapter will heal the frightened ego and bring peace and relief to the soul.

If your problem is something you did that was negative and causes you distress when you think about it, the angels will gently heal the pain and bring forgiveness to your heart. If you are hanging on to the pain and upsetting yourself, just imagine if somebody else had done the same thing. Would you think so badly of them? Would you be more understanding if a friend confided in you about something they had done that they were ashamed of? The answer is probably yes, for we can forgive others for their mistakes but rarely feel the same kind of sympathy for ourselves for similar errors of judgment. We all make mistakes and do things we later regret, but there is no point in dwelling on them and ruining our lives over them. The past is the past and no longer exists except in our minds.

We often forgive others much more easily than we are willing to forgive ourselves. We are also much more willing to be understanding of others than of ourselves. Such negative emotions can cause serious blocks on the spiritual path and need to be dealt with. This is where angel healing is so important, for it helps ease the pain of the ego and bring healing to a tortured heart. Angel healing helps us put the past behind us and see things in a new perspective. If we feel guilty because we hurt someone, it can be helpful to hold that person in angel light as a way of making amends. See the person surrounded by angels and flooded with their light. Then put the whole incident out of your mind. The angels will bring a wonderful healing to your heart, and who knows what it will do for the other person!

The meditation with the Powers angels in this chapter will bring sympathy and love for yourself to your heart and a deeper understanding of why you acted as you did. Forgiveness will come with the help of the angels, and you will find a new peace and tranquility in your soul replacing the blockages that were keeping you from realizing your true potential as a spiritual being.

If the blockage is caused by something that was done to you, the meditation with the Powers angels will bring about an understanding and a forgiveness that you thought were not possible. Letting go is the only route to take if you are to move on from what happened, and as I have already said, why let this person or persons have control of your life forever? Forgive and understand and release all the negative emotions that block your happiness. The angels are always by your side to offer support and love and will bring you the strength you need to heal your heart and soul.

PRAYER TO THE POWERS ANGELS

Dearest Powers angels, I thank you for the work you do to bring healing to human hearts and pray that your healing light will fill me and eradicate all blockages that prevent me from moving on. Bring love and forgiveness to my heart where it is needed and lead me to a place of peace and contentment.

MEDITATION WITH THE POWERS ANGELS TO REMOVE NEGATIVE BLOCKS

Sit before your angel altar and light your candle, reminding yourself that the flame represents the light at the very center of your being, which is the light of God. Relax yourself as detailed in chapter 2, and say the prayer to the Powers angel. Imagine yourself in your temple, and see your Guardian Angel waiting for you there. He or she stands behind you enveloping you in a radiant glow, ready to give you support and understanding during the meditation. Look around your temple and notice the colors and design to really focus your mind and switch off your everyday thoughts. Imagine before you a magnificent angel radiating a wonderful rose-colored light. This light floods your whole being and brings a gentle peace and happiness and a feeling of safety and security.

Feel the light filling you with love for yourself and all creation. Hold in your mind the incident that worries you, but try to feel detached from it. Feel the angel's power surging through you, clearing the blockages this incident causes and filling you instead with love, understanding, and forgiveness. If another person is involved whom you find difficult to forgive, use the figure-eight meditation with the Throne angels detailed in chapter 10. Imagine a figure eight made of light laid out before you. You are sitting in one circle, and opposite you in the other circle of the figure eight sits the person you wish to forgive. At the intersection stands the Powers angel enveloping both of you in a beautiful light. The angel holds a large sword, which he raises and brings down in a very definite manner, cutting the ties that have kept you locked together. Know that healing will take place within you and you will come to terms with whatever happened. You feel full of love for yourself and forgiveness for the other person involved. It is all in the past, and you now look forward to a happy and positive future free from distress and negative emotions.

If you really find it difficult to forgive the person, imagine giving all your negative emotions to the angel. Imagine the feelings as a dark cloud that you lift from your soul and hand over to the angel, who takes the cloud and enfolds you in a warm golden light of love and healing. The angel will help you overcome and release these negative emotions and move on to a much happier and fulfilling life. By repeating this meditation, you will gradually come to a place of forgiveness and find contentment in your heart.

Hold the feeling of angel love enfolding you for as long as is comfortable, and then bring your attention back to your actual surroundings. Close down your chakras as detailed in chapter 2, and take a sip of water to further ground yourself. You feel a great sense of release and relief and know that from now on you will face the future with a positive and courageous heart. All is well, and the past no longer has any hold over you.

Give thanks to the Powers angel for the wonderful feeling of release and for the healing love the angel has given you. Know in your heart that you forgive, whether it is yourself or someone else. The healing that has taken place is on a deep soul level and enables you to move on with a happy, contented heart.

Chapter 16

PRINCIPALITY ANGELS:
HELPING ENDANGERED SPECIES

Animal welfare is an issue that is close to the hearts of many people, especially the protection of endangered species whose very existence is threatened by poachers or destruction of habitat. Principality angels work tirelessly to help protect endangered species and have in their care the welfare of all animal life, including birds and marine life. They do this by giving help and support to all those organizations and individuals who work to protect animals that are endangered for whatever reason. They also work on the hearts of those who poach and hunt various species and endanger their survival in the wild.

If this is a subject to which you feel a particular affinity, then working with the Principality angels will bring joy and satisfaction to your heart. There are many species that are endangered in the world for various reasons, such as hunting by humankind or diminishing habitats due to human encroachment.

There is still, unfortunately, a lot of cruelty shown toward animals, and the Principality angels work to bring love and healing to the hearts of humankind. There are many organizations that work for the welfare of animals and indeed all wildlife, and Principality angels give them their love and support.

Angels never sit in judgment of humans, but lovingly and ceaselessly work to rectify the mistakes that we make. It is possible to work closely with the Principality angels to help heal the harm done to certain animal species, and this can be very fulfilling work. The Principality angels work to help all living species on the planet, including insects, reptiles, fish, whales, mammals, and birds. Their work also includes giving healing power to those organizations and sanctuaries that take in abandoned and neglected animals. This work is very close to my heart, and I find great joy and satisfaction working with the angels in this way.

To join in this work, meditate with the Principality angels to help the organizations that work so tirelessly for endangered and vulnerable wildlife and all those organizations that work to help and heal animals that have been mistreated. This will only take about ten minutes a day and will be very worthwhile work. I do this work with the Principality angels once a week at a regular time and it brings me great satisfaction, for I know the angel power is helping and healing somewhere in the world.

PRAYER TO THE PRINCIPALITIES

Dearest Principality angels, we give thanks for the work you do with endangered and vulnerable wildlife. We pray that we will bring extra power to your work to assist those organizations and sanctuaries that work ceaselessly to help wildlife, and know that your loving power is constantly flowing to them.

MEDITATION WITH THE PRINCIPALITIES TO HELP ENDANGERED SPECIES

Sit comfortably with your back straight in front of your angel altar, and take a few deep breaths. Light your candle and focus on the flame, remembering that it represents the spark of God within. Say the prayer to the Principality angels, and then do the relaxation exercise as described in chapter 2. When you feel ready, imagine yourself in your inner temple next to your Guardian Angel, who is ready to provide support for the work you are about to do.

Imagine before you the Principality angel bathed in a beautiful rose-colored light. This light is very powerful, and you see it radiating out to fill your temple. This glorious light also fills every cell of your being, so feel it radiating from yourself out into the wider world. If you have a particular cause or organization that you hold dear to your heart, now is the time to concentrate on it for a few moments and see the light of the angel enfolding all the workers and the animals they support. Be aware of the light going into the world to empower all organizations that work for the good of all endangered species, and know that this work really does help those involved in this cause. See also the light enfolding vulnerable species who may be under stress due to climatic changes or the encroachment of their habitats by humans.

Hold yourself in this beautiful light, and feel it spreading around the world for as long as you feel comfortable. Then bring your attention back to your actual surroundings. Take a few deep breaths, then close down your chakras as detailed in chapter 2. Take a few sips of water to fully ground yourself.

You will find this work particularly satisfying if you feel deeply for the welfare of animals and all wildlife. As I have said, I do this meditation once a week at the same time on the same day so that the mind really gets used to the regularity of the work. This will help focus the mind more acutely for the work you undertake and make it that much more powerful.

Chapter 17

PRINCIPALITY ANGELS:
PROMOTING HUMAN RIGHTS AND ERADICATING DISCRIMINATION

If promoting human rights is a cause that is close to your heart, the Principality angels are the ones to work with. You may think that there is nothing you can do to help on the physical level except perhaps by supporting organizations that campaign for human rights. But here is something very valuable you can do to help these organizations, and that is to hold them in the light of the Principality angels, whose power will greatly strengthen the work they do.

Principalities assist those organizations that campaign for human rights and those that work to eradicate discrimination in all its forms. If you feel discriminated against, these are the angels to ask for help in the situation.

In cases of discrimination for any reason, be it race, age, gender, or religion, learning to forgive and understanding that discrimination is rooted in ignorance and fear is a valuable undertaking that can lessen the hurt that such attitudes cause. Everyone has the same spark of the Divine within and is entitled to be treated with fairness and respect.

It is important not to get too negative about the discrimination but instead to remain detached. Don't give that person extra power over you by getting angry. The hurt and pain such situations bring can be relieved by letting go of any emotional attachment, such as anger, and seeing the person or persons responsible in the light of forgiveness. This may be very hard to do, but it will ease the hurt, and angels can help a great deal in these situations. Hold yourself in the light of the Principality angels, a beautiful rose-colored light, and you will feel safe and uplifted, and any pain you feel will be eased by these powerful angels.

The angels can help by subtly bringing a change of attitude to the person responsible by holding the person in their light. The meditation with the Principality angels in this chapter will also help you a great deal by giving you the courage to forgive and take whatever action is necessary, whether this be reporting the situation to a superior if the discrimination takes place at work or taking legal action if you feel you have been grossly undermined in some way.

Whatever course of action you take, as long as it is done in a positive manner, the angels will be by your side to help and give you the courage to continue. It may be that you need to speak out to defend yourself, in which case you should envelop yourself in the light of the Principality angels to protect yourself and hold the other person in angel light as well to make the situation as positive as possible.

Even in our so-called civilized world, there is still a great deal of discrimination that brings great harm to many people. This can even be between various sects of the same religion or, as in Africa, between differing tribes. The work you do with the Principality angels will help bring about an understanding and heighten awareness of the divine spark within, leading to the knowledge that we are all one in the eyes of God. Discrimination usually stems from fear—a fear that whatever or whoever is different from ourselves must be threatening in some way. The Principality angels strive tirelessly to bring to the human heart the understanding that there is nothing to fear from people who seem on the surface to be different from ourselves. They work continuously to bring awareness that it is the ego that fears that which is different and that on the soul level there are no differences, for we all come from the same divine source. The Principality angels can bring the recognition that we are all the same beneath the ego, and there is nothing to fear. The angels' love will open up the hearts of all humankind to the divine power and the knowledge that we are all one.

There are many places in the world where human rights are an issue, and it is very worthwhile work to hold these places in the light of angels to bring healing to human souls and to help bring about justice and understanding. Disregard for human rights usually comes from fear of losing power in some way, but the angels work ceaselessly to help those who are hurt by such attitudes to find healing and strength. The angels also work on the hearts of the perpetrators of such actions, and you can work with the angels to bring their healing love and light into the world to eradicate this disregard for fellow human beings. This is some of the most important work you can do with angels. If performed with a genuine loving heart, such work can bring great joy to the spirit within.

PRAYER TO THE PRINCIPALITIES

Dearest Principality angels, we give thanks for your work and pray that our efforts in working with you will bring relief and aid in those areas in the world where human rights are an issue. We pray also that your light will shine on negative attitudes and that we will be able to find forgiveness in our hearts where there is pain and anger.

Meditation with the Principalities to Promote Human Rights

Light a candle and sit comfortably in front of your altar with your back straight and your hands held loosely in your lap. Concentrate on the flame of the candle, and remember that it is a symbol of the light within you that is a spark of God. This spark within you does not know discrimination and can bring healing to the most difficult of situations. Through the meditation with the angels it will grow and give you courage and inspiration, and maybe you will find it in your heart to forgive.

Say the prayer to the Principality angels, then take a few deep breaths and do the relaxation exercise as detailed in chapter 2. Imagine yourself in your temple, where your Guardian Angel awaits you. He or she stands behind you with hands resting on your shoulders to give you support during the meditation.

See before you a most beautiful angel bathed in rose-colored light, the color of love and healing. This light fills your temple and envelops you in a warm glow.

If you wish to help human rights organizations, visualize the rose-colored light enfolding the symbol or the name of the organization you wish to help. If there is a place in the world where discrimination against groups of people particularly upsets you, hold this area in the light of the angels or say the name of the groups of people that are involved. You may feel that you cannot possibly be providing any real help, but rest assured that this is a very powerful meditation and your help will be received somewhere in the world. See the rose-colored light of the angel radiating out from your temple into the world, where it heals the darkness caused by fear and ignorance. Hold this vision for as long as is comfortable, and then bring your awareness back to your actual surroundings. Close your chakras as detailed in chapter 2, and take a few sips of water to completely ground yourself.

If personal discrimination is a problem for you, feel the rose-colored light of the Principality angel enfolding you and filling every cell of your being with comfort and love.

Feel this love giving you the courage and confidence to take whatever steps are necessary.

Then visualize a figure eight made of the rose-colored light, with the angel standing at the intersection of the two circles. You are seated in the lower half of the figure, and the person or persons you have the problem with are seated in the upper half of the figure. The angel enfolds all of you in the powerful rose-colored light, and you know that whatever action you need to take, all will be well. The light gives you courage to stand up for yourself in a positive manner to resolve the situation.

Hold this vision for as long as you feel comfortable, and then bring your awareness back to your actual surroundings. Thank the angel for his or her help in bringing healing comfort to your situation. Close your chakras as detailed in chapter 2, and take a few sips of water to further ground yourself. Know that all will be well and that you will have the courage and all the help you need from the angels to deal with the problem in a positive and just way.

Chapter 18

PRINCIPALITY ANGELS:
BRINGING POSITIVE ENERGY TO TOWNS AND CITIES

Living in the depths of the countryside as I do, I used to think of large towns and cities as rather negative places, and when visiting a place such as London, I would be aware of negative energy and hold myself in a bubble of protective light. Still, although a lot of negativity exists in cities, they are also places of extreme positive energy.

If you live in a city, you will be aware of the vibrant energy that radiates throughout the place and know how exciting and exhilarating urban life can be. A city is a place where people can prosper and develop, a place of abundant opportunities and positive creative activities. There is no doubt that there is also a fair amount of negative energy in a city, which is no surprise given the population levels. It would be surprising if there was no negativity.

The energy of a city can be very creative and uplifting. Cities can make loneliness more acutely felt, but they are also places where there are many opportunities to meet people and make positive friendships. There is also a lot of nature in cities, for most cities have parks and gardens where there is abundant wildlife. Angels of all varieties work in cities to bring the greatest number of opportunities to those living there, to look after the wildlife, and to uplift and inspire all human activity.

Each city has its own special angel, or deva, of the Principality hierarchy who looks after the whole city and who has in his or her care all the various angels who work in different aspects in the city. This angel is very powerful and all-seeing and can be called upon to promote positive energy wherever it is needed. This beautiful angel works constantly to combat the negative energy of the city and endeavors to bring forth the positive goodness of all citizens in a creative and harmonious way.

If you live in a city, tune in to this angel and feel the vibrant energy that radiates from him or her. This energy will uplift you and protect you from the negative forces that unfortunately are all too prevalent in places where large numbers of human beings live together in close proximity.

Each town or village also has an individual angel that oversees the area. So wherever you live, tune in to your "local" deva and experience the positive energy that is creative and uplifting and is there for everyone who lives in the area.

The purpose of these devas is to promote harmony and community spirit among the inhabitants and to combat the negative forces that prevail. Human beings are very vulnerable to negative forces, and you can help the angels to overcome these by tuning in to them and radiating their light and love to your surroundings. By tuning in to these angels, you also open yourself to their creative and inspirational energy, which they are forever radiating to influence all those who are aware of angel power. Cities and towns abound with creative energy, and it is fair to say that there is far more positive energy in cities and towns than there is negative energy, but unfortunately it is the negative happenings that news programs and individuals tend to focus on.

Living in the country, I am very aware of nature angels. While I experience the tranquility and beauty of the countryside, such peace and tranquility can also be found in cities and towns if you appreciate and use the open spaces of parks and gardens. When visiting a park, be aware of the nature angels who are at work there. By tuning in to their beauty, you will find peace and inspiration and bring a positive nourishment to your soul. Tuning in to the angels' tranquility is an activity that can be experienced anywhere, regardless of your surroundings. Appreciation of beauty can also be heightened in the city, for if you look for it, there is beauty everywhere. Try walking along your street and counting how many beautiful things there are, and really appreciate them. It will make your life richer, as the more aware you are of beauty, the more you will see it.

The following meditation will lead you to a place of peace and comfort and bring a keen awareness of the positive possibilities a city or town has to offer. Perform it once a week on a regular basis to get the utmost help in living harmoniously in your environment. By tuning in to the angels, you can help in their work of bringing positive energy to overcome negative forces and help bring awareness of the creative and social opportunities that towns and cities have to offer.

Prayer to the Principalities

Dearest Principality angels, we give thanks for the work you do to make towns and cities safer places by combating negative forces. We pray that our work with you will help overcome these negative forces and bring about an awareness of the positive creative aspects that flourish everywhere in this town (city).

Meditation with the Principalities for Positive Energy in Cities

Sit comfortably with your back straight in front of your angel altar. Light your candle and remind yourself that the flame represents the spark of God that dwells deep within you. Say the prayer to the Principality angels, then relax yourself as detailed in chapter 2. Imagine yourself in your inner temple, where your Guardian Angel greets you with arms outstretched to enfold you in glorious light. With your Guardian Angel beside you, imagine before you a beautiful angel of golden light. Feel this light enfolding you and filling every cell of your being. Imagine this light filling your whole temple and radiating out into your physical surroundings. See this light in all its creative and positive power enfolding the whole of the city or town where you live and bringing light to all who live there.

This will have a very positive and creative effect. Be aware that many people will be touched by the light of the angel. Your work will bring much-needed positivity to many areas of city or town life, and many people will be touched by angel magic, which will work miracles in their lives.

Hold this feeling for as long as you are able, and then bring your awareness back to your physical surroundings. Close down your chakras as detailed in chapter 2, and take a few sips of water to further ground yourself. Give thanks to the angel for his or her tireless work to make towns and cities safe and positive places to live. You may feel there is too much negative energy in urban areas for your work to be of use, but those who are open to positive forces *will* be touched by the wings of angels and will feel their love and support.

Chapter 19

ARCHANGEL MICHAEL:
PROTECTING THE WEAK
AND FIGHTING INJUSTICE

Perhaps archangels are the best known of all the angels, for they are the ones who have appeared most often to humankind with messages from the Divine. There are said to be seven archangels, each with different attributes. Archangels are very powerful angels. Working with them is particularly satisfying and will bring a great love to your heart and wisdom to your soul.

Archangels are more concerned with individual healing, so you should find an archangel that relates to your particular problem. Archangel Michael is the exception, for he protects the weak in the world. There are many in the world who are vulnerable due to exploitation, poverty, and dictatorships and feel too intimidated to voice their concerns. Injustice can happen to anyone at any time, and it often seems that there is nothing one can do about it. The perpetrators of injustice seem to get away with it. But in reality, no one can get away with creating injustice, for all of us are subject to the divine law of cause and effect, or karma. But that does not help their victims, who may be left hurt and distressed by their actions.

Archangel Michael works tirelessly to protect the weak and vulnerable, and to join in this work will bring untold joy to your heart. He does not sit in judgment of those people who abuse their positions of power, but holds them also in the light of the Divine. Forgiveness is as much a part of the healing process as is the work of the angels. Those who are old and vulnerable to the negative actions of others are also held in the light of the angels, as are victims of abuse and crime. Children are particularly vulnerable to the abusive actions of others, often by those who should be protecting them. The list of those who are "weak" is a long one. Being a dedicated worker on the earth plane gives so much more power to the work of Michael in his never-ceasing work of protecting the weak.

You would probably agree that there seems to be a great deal of injustice in the world, and you may feel helpless to solve problems of injustice, especially if it happens to you. But you have more power than you realize, for helping Archangel Michael to fight injustice in the world is one of the most important and powerful things you can do.

Giving aid or volunteer hours to organizations that work for the relief of those who are vulnerable is one way to help, but if you are not able to work with them on a practical level, working with them on a spiritual level is another very powerful way to help. Practice the meditation in this chapter of holding all workers for injustice in the light of the Archangel Michael, and he will send his love and power to such organizations to help in the battle against injustice in the world.

Intimidation of the weak and vulnerable is a contemptible crime, and if you feel helpless against such things, practicing the healing meditation with Archangel Michael is something very tangible that you can do. You may think that a little meditation for a few minutes a day cannot achieve very much, but never underestimate the power of the angels, especially that of Archangel Michael, for someone, somewhere, will be touched by his power and his love, and there will be just that little bit less injustice in the world.

If you feel you have been the victim of an injustice, hold yourself in the light of Archangel Michael and he will bring his healing power to your soul. He does not sit in judgment of anyone, so revenge is not an option! But his love and power can bring about a resolution and help bring forgiveness to your heart, which is the one sure route to positive healing. If forgiveness is too difficult, just hold yourself in the light of Michael and you will feel a healing balm radiating throughout your body and soul. Hold the person or persons responsible for the injustice in the light as well, and this will help bring a positive outcome to the problem.

Prayer to Archangel Michael

Archangel Michael, we give thanks for your work in protecting the weak and pray that our own work with you will contribute to the healing you bring to so many people. May the light of goodness and justice shine from our hearts and mingle with your powerful light to help us hear the voices of those who suffer from injustice.

Meditation with Archangel Michael to Fight Injustice

Sit comfortably in front of your altar. If you wish, light your candle and concentrate for a while on the flame, which represents the light of the Divine in your heart. Say the prayer to Archangel Michael, and then do the relaxation exercise as detailed in chapter 2. Imagine yourself in your inner temple, where your Guardian Angel awaits you with love and support for the work you are about to undertake.

See before you the magnificent Archangel Michael. His golden light fills your temple and enfolds you in a warm feeling of love and happiness. Fill yourself with his light and see this light spreading out into the world, where so many need his protection and support. Don't dwell on any particular injustice, for Archangel Michael will know best where to direct the light. His light floods the whole world, and you can imagine this golden light encircling the globe, enfolding the whole earth in his light and protecting those who are so vulnerable and at risk. If you want to give help to a particular organization, see the name of that organization held in the light of Archangel Michael and know that his power is going to their workers in their fight against injustice.

Hold this image in your mind for as long as you feel comfortable, then bring your awareness back to your actual surroundings. Know that someone, somewhere, will be touched by the magic of Archangel Michael and that your work is not in vain, for you work from the spirit within, which is of God and is all-powerful.

Close your chakras as detailed in chapter 2, and take a sip of water to further ground yourself. Thank Archangel Michael for his work that is so needed in the world. You can repeat this meditation as often as you feel able. I usually perform it every other day, alternating with whatever meditation I particularly want to practice at any given time.

If you feel you have been the victim of some injustice, it is very healing to practice a meditation with Archangel Michael. Prepare yourself as before and see yourself in your temple surrounded by the loving, healing light of Archangel Michael. Imagine the light emanating from Michael as forming a figure eight. You are seated in one section, and the perpetrator or perpetrators of the injustice are in the other section. Archangel Michael stands at the intersection and holds a sword of light. See him bring the sword down three times to sever the link between you. This is a very powerful exercise and will bring a healing to your heart. It will also bring healing to the situation, and you will be surprised as to how the injustice is resolved.

It is important to close your chakras completely after this meditation, and as an extra measure of healing, hold yourself in the center of a cross of light within a circle of light. This is a powerful symbol of protection against negative power and will bring an added wisdom to your heart.

Chapter 20

ARCHANGEL RAPHAEL:
HEALING ILLNESS AND DISEASE

Illness of any kind can be frightening and demoralizing. Sometimes our fear can limit the healing process, and the negative attitude that fear brings can seriously hinder any healing from taking place. Archangel Raphael can help a great deal in this situation by stilling the fear and anger and bringing healing to your emotions and mental attitude as well as to your physical body. Raphael is a very powerful healer. Meditation with him will bring the healing power of the Divine to your body and also help dismiss the fear that serious illness can bring, bringing to your heart a new confidence in your recovery.

Angel healing should not be seen as a replacement for medical treatment but as something that goes hand in hand with medical help. Always consult a doctor if you feel unwell, but also practice the meditation with Archangel Raphael to bring extra healing power to whatever treatment you are receiving.

Spiritual healing works on a deep level, healing the soul where illness and disease first appear before manifesting in the physical body. Getting to the root cause of your illness can be very beneficial and will speed up the healing process. Archangel Raphael will heal the soul and thereby bring about a gentle healing to the body, and also bring a sense of calm and peace to a degree that you have not experienced before.

Angel healing with Raphael takes place on a very deep level and will enfold you with a love that will uplift and bring about confidence in your recovery. However down your illness makes you feel, know that the angels are with you to hold your hand and whisper words of encouragement. It may be difficult to live a normal life when you are ill, but Raphael will bring his strength and love to your physical being and you will find that life takes on a new meaning. Raphael will be with you, as will your Guardian

Angel, who never leaves your side but is always there to enfold you in healing love.

When my mother was very ill, I was talking with her doctor and I happened to mention that she was receiving spiritual healing. I thought he might be taken aback, but instead he said that it was the best healing she could receive. Believe in your healing and believe in the angels, for their healing is not something that is wishful thinking. Angel healing is very powerful and cuts through feelings of impatience and fear to bring you to a calm and joyful state of mind. When working with Archangel Raphael, you will find that all aspects of your life improve and not only your health, for he enfolds you in the most powerful healing love imaginable.

When you are feeling ill, it is not easy to meditate, but just ask for Archangel Raphael's help and he will be with you to give his love and healing. He emits a powerful silver light, the color of healing, and if you feel up to it, direct this light to where the dis-ease is in your body. Just imagine this beautiful angel standing in front of you directing a powerful ray of light to your problem area, and feel the light filling every cell of your being. Don't worry about trying too hard at this; the secret is to relax and not worry about the clarity of your visualization. Just thinking about Raphael will bring him to you with his healing power.

How long you can hold the visualization is of no importance either, for trying to hold it for a long time can cause tension and will hinder the healing power. Do a quick relaxation by relaxing your shoulders and your neck and facial muscles and give one really deep breath to release any tension you might be feeling. It is helpful to say an affirmation, such as "Divine light fills every cell of my being." Say this simple affirmation several times during the day to remind yourself of the healing power that flows to you from the angels. A very powerful affirmation is "The divine healing power of Archangel Raphael fills every cell of my being." Such affirmations will bring courage and strength to the soul and will allow the healing power of Raphael to flow into the physical body.

If you feel able, the following meditation with Raphael will help enormously to give you confidence that all will be well and the knowledge that healing *can* take place.

Prayer to Archangel Raphael

Dearest Archangel Raphael, I give thanks for the healing power of the Divine that you are able to bring to humankind. May you bring your healing to my soul and body and eradicate the dis-ease that I have. I give thanks for your help in my time of need.

Meditation with Archangel Raphael to Heal the Body

Sit comfortably in a place where you will be warm and cozy. You need not have your altar in front of you if it is inconvenient. If convenient, light a candle. Otherwise, imagine a little flame to remind yourself of the power of the Divine that dwells within. Say the prayer to Archangel Raphael, then take a few deep breaths to calm yourself and do the relaxation exercise detailed in chapter 2. When relaxed, imagine yourself in your inner temple. Your Guardian Angel is there enfolding you with the rose-colored light of love. He or she stands behind you with hands on your shoulders to give you support.

Imagine a magnificent angel before you radiating a silver light. This angel envelops you in love, and the silver light penetrates your whole being—body, soul, and mind. Feel the silver light radiating throughout your body, easing away dis-ease and restoring a healthy balance to your body. If there is a particular place in your body that needs healing, see Archangel Raphael direct a powerful silver ray to that area and know that healing on a deep level will take place. All fear is extinguished with the power of Raphael, whose healing love gives you a deep peace and knowledge that all is well.

As I mentioned in the chapter on Guardian Angels (chapter 4), green is also a very healing color because of its cleansing power. It is especially good for healing infections of any kind, and I have often used this color when I have a cold.

If you are suffering from an infection, imagine Archangel Raphael radiating a beautiful green light that floods your whole body. This is very cleansing, and it melts away any infection you are suffering from. It is also a strengthening light. When flooding your body, it gives you the strength to naturally fight off the infection. Hold yourself in this green light for as long as you feel able, and know that a gentle healing is taking place.

When you feel ready, bring your awareness back to your actual surroundings and take a few deep breaths. Close your chakras as detailed in chapter 2, then take a sip of water to fully ground yourself. Give thanks to Archangel Raphael for the healing love he has given you, and feel at peace with yourself.

The healing power of Raphael can also be sent to someone you know who may need healing. It is possible to send healing love to anyone, and it is a very simple exercise to do.

This is lovely work and can bring a great peace and satisfaction to the soul. Spiritual healing works on many different levels and brings a great sense of well-being to your own soul. Send this healing by performing the following meditation, and know that healing love from Archangel Raphael will bring peace and healing to that soul.

PRAYER TO ARCHANGEL RAPHAEL

Dearest Archangel Raphael, we give thanks for your healing power that comes directly from the Divine and pray that your healing love be sent to (say the name of the person you wish to send healing to). May your healing power bring well-being to this soul and a deep sense of peace and acceptance.

MEDITATION WITH ARCHANGEL RAPHAEL TO SEND HEALING POWER

Sit before your altar and make sure you are comfortable and warm. Light your candle to remind yourself of the spark of God deep within you. This spark of the Divine also has the power to heal when lit by the power of Archangel Raphael. Take a few deep breaths, then do the relaxation exercise as detailed in chapter 2. Close your eyes and imagine yourself in your inner temple, where your Guardian Angel awaits you with arms outstretched in loving greeting. He or she enfolds you in golden light. Your Guardian Angel then stands behind you with hands on your shoulders to give you support.

Imagine before you the beautiful form of Archangel Raphael radiating a silver or green light (whichever color you feel is most appropriate). Then imagine the person to whom you wish to send the healing also standing before you, bathed in the healing light of Raphael. See the light enfolding and permeating every cell of the person's being, and know that the healing love of Raphael is bringing health and vitality back to that person. Hold this image for as long as is comfortable, and then bring your awareness back to your actual surroundings. Take a few deep breaths, then close down your chakras as detailed in chapter 2. Take a few sips of water to further ground yourself, and don't forget to put out your candle!

You may think that your healing efforts will not possibly have any effect, but that is to doubt the power of the angels and the power of the Divine. Rest assured that healing *will* take place on some level of the psyche, for work with the angels is never a waste.

ANIMAL HEALING WITH ARCHANGEL RAPHAEL

The healing power of Raphael can also help animals, so if you know of a pet that is unwell, you can also hold them in the healing light of Raphael. Animals are very responsive to spiritual healing, and it is very satisfying work to do.

If you can actually have physical contact with the animal in question, tune in to Archangel Raphael and ask for his help. This help will immediately be at hand, and Raphael will be ready to enfold the animal and yourself in love and healing. Imagine Raphael before you enfolding you in silver or green light and then see this light glowing brightly in your hand. Place your hand on the head of the animal and work down the spine, seeing the light of Raphael flooding the animal's body. Have belief in the work you are doing, for it will bring about a beautiful healing. Quietly thank Archangel Raphael for being there and giving his healing help to your animal friend.

If you do not have contact with the animal, you can do a meditation to send healing light to the animal in question. Prepare yourself as before and imagine yourself in your inner temple, where your Guardian Angel welcomes you with love. See Archangel Raphael before you holding the particular sick animal in his arms. Raphael is surrounded by a beautiful and powerful light of either silver or green, and he gently enfolds the animal in this light. See the light flooding the entire body of the sick animal, restoring health and well-being. When you feel ready, let the image fade and bring your awareness back to your actual surroundings. Close down your chakras as detailed in chapter 2, and know that your work with Raphael will have a definite effect.

I performed the healing exercise with Raphael on my own cats with very positive results. However, when my dear Pepper had a tumor, full healing was not to be, although I am sure the healing that Raphael sent to her did ease her suffering. She was quite old for a cat, so it was time for her to pass on. The loving care of Raphael helped me during this time and brought about a calm acceptance. I know that when she did pass over, she was taken into the care of the angels and did not suffer in any way.

Whatever healing you wish to share with Archangel Raphael, whether it be for yourself, for another person, or for an animal, know that healing on some level will take place and suffering will be minimized. Know also that the love of the angels is always with you whatever the outcome of your efforts and that the love of the angels will bring about newfound vitality and joy to your innermost being.

Because of his powerful healing energy, Raphael is also the angel to work with where there is famine or disease in the world. His love and power will bring help to such situations and relief to those involved. Imagine the area that is affected and visualize it flooded with the healing light of Raphael. Know that his power and wisdom are bringing much-needed help to all who suffer. His healing power will also bring assistance to those organizations that work for the relief of famine and disease in the world, bringing fresh energy and determination to all who work in such groups. This is very valuable work to do and will bring deep satisfaction to the spirit.

Chapter 21

ARCHANGEL URIEL:
FINDING DIRECTION IN LIFE
AND FOLLOWING YOUR DREAMS

If you come to a point in life where you don't know what to do or which way to turn, Archangel Uriel is the angel to ask for help, for his great love and wisdom will guide you to do what is right and positive.

If you find yourself in a situation where you need ideas, Uriel will give you that inspiration. There are many situations in life where inspiration is needed or a fresh approach is required because your life is getting stale or not going as well as you had hoped. You might well find yourself in a situation where you feel stuck in a way of living that you know is not right for you, but you can see no way out and all ways out are blocked for some reason. Your life seems dull and lacking in purpose. You have dreams of how you would like to be living, but these dreams seem unobtainable. Such a negative way of life can be soul-destroying, especially if you cannot see how to change things for the better. This is where the power of Archangel Uriel will help, for he can bring fresh ideas and illuminate ways of living that you perhaps had not thought of. Archangel Uriel can unblock that which seems hopeless and show the way to a more positive and happier way of life.

Sometimes being stuck in a rut can feel like a safe option in life, and any changes to routine can seem scary, even though you know that change is the right thing for you. Archangel Uriel will give you the courage to take steps to change your life and follow your dreams with a positive outlook.

Life should feel good and positive, and it is our birthright to feel joy and happiness in our daily living, so if your life does not reflect these states of being, if life is dull, then a radical change is the only way forward. Angels are always by your side to support you in your endeavors and point the way to a better way of living. Archangel Uriel is there for you to help you achieve your dreams in life and find the direction you are lacking. He is beside you to whisper words of encouragement and bring inspiration. He will bring fresh ideas and hope and help you find the correct path to living a happy and joyful life.

You may know that change is important in your life, but if you are overworked and stressed, sometimes it is difficult to see the forest from the trees. Uriel will bring a deep peace to your heart and mind and help you see which is the best path forward for you.

You may know what you wish to achieve in life but don't know how to achieve those dreams. Archangel Uriel can make your dreams come true. He can unlock the great power that is the truth of your being and set you on the path to success and prosperity. Whatever you dream of, it can become a reality with the help of Archangel Uriel, who will be with you every step of the way showing you the right course to take. He will give you the courage to take the first step to realizing your dream and to continue pursuing your dream with a positive heart.

Sometimes it is difficult to see which course of action would be the best to take when several are offered to you. Again, Archangel Uriel can help by guiding you to the option that will have the most positive effect in your life. Sometimes in life you come to a crossroads, where two different paths, or more, are open to you and you don't know which option to choose. All routes may look good, and worry can set in as to which way to go. Thoughts go round and round in your head over the advantages and disadvantages of the different paths that could be taken. Potential opportunities lost if you take the wrong way come to mind, and this can intensify the worry even further and cause distressing confusion in your mind.

Archangel Uriel can bring peace to the worried and confused mind and shine a light of clarity upon the situation, thereby showing a clear way of progress.

Archangel Uriel has the wisdom to know what is best for you and can see the situation from a different viewpoint. He can see all angles and the results of taking different routes, and he knows what will bring the greatest happiness to you and what will have the most profound effect on your life. He will show you the safest and most appropriate course to take, a path that will bring rewards of great happiness and contentment. If you find yourself with several options, just imagine a great angel in front of you and send him your love, and then ask what is the correct path to follow. This will be Archangel Uriel, and he will guide you to the best way to move forward. Think of each option in turn and feel your reaction to each in your solar plexus. Archangel Uriel will guide you by making you feel really good about one particular option, which you will instinctively know is right for you. Make changes to your life with the confidence that with the help of the angels you have made the right decision and have the courage to follow Archangel Uriel's guidance.

Alternatively, keep a notebook handy, for you might receive messages in the form of thoughts as to why a particular choice is right for you or why it is not such a good idea. Trust the angels and you will find yourself on a pathway to success and happiness.

Meditation with Archangel Uriel will bring his great love and power to guide you to make the best decision and ensure that you take the most advantageous route.

If a radical change is called for in your life because you feel stuck in a situation that seemingly has no way out, try the meditation in this chapter and you will find yourself inspired to try new things that bring about a positive and happier pathway in life, one that is right for you, bringing a fulfillment and joy you may once have thought impossible. Archangel Uriel will also provide you with the courage to take the necessary steps to achieve this new way of life, and by working with Archangel Uriel, you will soon find that your life becomes fulfilling and very exciting! This is the truth of working with angels. You will find that angel power can bring the most surprising results that are never boring but are always exciting!

I do the meditation in this chapter when I feel I have lost my direction and am making no progress in achieving my goals in life. It always helps me to make a breakthrough and set me on a positive path. If I have a particular goal I want to achieve but don't know where to start, I practice this meditation to give me the courage and inspiration to move forward.

Sometimes it can be scary to make a big change in your life and to take the first steps to realizing your dreams, but the meditation with Archangel Uriel will help give you the courage and determination to start on the path to happiness, success, and prosperity.

You need to have a very clear idea of what your dreams are in order to realize them. Sometimes we have a vague idea of what we would like to be doing, but to make dreams come true, you need to focus on them with clarity. As you go about your daily business, keep a positive thought in your mind about what you wish to achieve, and with the help of Archangel Uriel, you will soon be on the way to making your dream a reality. For the purposes of this meditation, have a clear thought or image in your

mind that represents your dream, and focus the light of
Archangel Uriel upon it.

Prayer to Archangel Uriel

Dearest Archangel Uriel, show me the right path in life,
one that will bring upliftment to my soul and inspire my
spirit. Shine your light on my life and my dreams. Bring
direction where there is none and answers where I have
questions.

Meditation with Archangel Uriel to Find Direction in Life

Prepare yourself by sitting comfortably in front of your
altar, and breathe deeply for a few moments. Light your
candle and concentrate on the flame, remembering that it
represents the spark of the Divine with you. Then say the
prayer to Archangel Uriel and perform the relaxation exercise as detailed in chapter 2. Close your eyes and imagine
yourself in your inner temple, where your Guardian Angel
welcomes you with love and warmth and stands beside you
ready to give you help and support.

See before you a beautiful angel bathed in a beautiful
green and golden light. This light radiates forth from the
angel and enfolds you. The green light cleanses away the

dullness and negativity that are so stifling to your spirit, and the golden light brings inspiration and wisdom to set you on the right path. This new pathway will bring the greatest happiness and joy to your life. Feel the glorious golden light of Uriel filling every cell of your being, bringing fresh ideas for a new way of living. You feel at peace with yourself and know that from now on your life will be fulfilling and you will have the joy of feeling alive. Uriel's wisdom enables you to make the right decisions to bring about positive change and the fulfillment of your dearest dreams. Feel this golden light illuminating your whole being, and know that all is well in your life.

If you have a particular dream you wish to work on, shine the golden light of Archangel Uriel on the image that represents it, or hold the clear thought of the dream in your mind as you bathe yourself in the golden light of the Archangel.

Hold yourself in the light of Archangel Uriel for as long as you feel able, then bring your awareness back to your actual surroundings. Take a few deep breaths, then close your chakras as detailed in chapter 2. Take a few sips of water to fully ground yourself. Give thanks to Archangel Uriel for his help at this time in your life, and send him your love by radiating a rose-colored ray of light from your heart or by saying the words "My love to you, dear Archangel Uriel," whichever you feel most comfortable with.

Have a notebook and pen handy to jot down any ideas that come to you. Ideas will definitely come to you about how you can change your life for the better and achieve your goals in life that have been eluding you. If you are faced with several choices about the direction to go in, think about each option in turn. You will feel a surge of joy when you come to the one that is best for you, or you will feel stronger about one course of action than others. This can happen immediately after the meditation or over the next few days. Be aware of your feelings, and jot down any ideas. Know that Archangel Uriel and your Guardian Angel are right by your side to support you as you go about making changes to your life. You may need to practice this meditation a few times before definite ideas come to you, but don't give up, for angel power will never let you down. Know that there are exciting times ahead!

Repeat the meditation until you feel you are well on your way to achieving your goals, then practice the meditation with Archangel Gabriel in the next chapter. Archangel Gabriel is the angel to ask for help when you are going through a major change in your life. His love and power will ensure that all runs smoothly and positively. He and Archangel Uriel will be with you throughout your journey to give their love and support as you move toward completion of your dreams.

Chapter 22

ARCHANGEL GABRIEL:
MAKING MAJOR CHANGES IN LIFE WITH EASE

Even with the help of angels, making major changes in your life can be daunting and they can fill your mind with doubts and misgivings about whether you are doing the right thing. You can be particularly vulnerable at such times and open to negative conditions, but asking Archangel Gabriel for his guidance and help will greatly assist you in facing the changes that need to be made and give you protection from any negative influences. His love and power can help things run smoothly and can help you feel calm and have the strength to cope with the transition period.

If you have been practicing the meditation with Archangel Uriel seeking direction in life from chapter 21 and are now prepared to make major changes to your life and need the courage to put your ideas into action, then Archangel Gabriel is the angel to seek to help you on your journey.

Major changes can be very positive and exciting, but it is still advisable to seek the power of the angels to bring their positive influence to bear on the situation.

Perhaps the change in your life is very challenging and is causing you some trepidation, and you are not sure what the future will bring. This may be starting a new job, moving to a new area, having a baby, or ending a relationship that you are no longer happy with. Whatever the change is, angels will be by your side to uplift and guide you and give their love to assist you in adapting to your new situation.

Major change can be quite stressful, but Archangel Gabriel will surround you in his protecting love and ensure that all changes run smoothly in your life. When Archangel Gabriel is actively involved in your life, there is no need for concern that change will be anything but positive. His love and power will protect you and ensure that you make the right decisions. The changes you make will be exciting and worthwhile and will bring about good fortune and all that you hoped for.

Change in your life can also bring changes in your relationships, for people can react when friends or relatives make a major change in their lives. Often, friends or relatives are very positive and supportive, but sometimes they feel quite threatened and then react negatively. Archangel Gabriel is always by your side when you tune in to him, and he will help you deal with these situations. Change in your life can be quite frightening for others who perhaps feel that their own way of life is being challenged. Archangel Gabriel will give you the wisdom to heal these negative feelings in others and also the courage to show your joy at the changes you are making. If someone does react in a negative way, just hold them in the light of Archangel Gabriel and you will be surprised at how quickly their reaction becomes one of positive support!

The following meditation with Archangel Gabriel will help at all times in your life when a major change is happening.

Prayer to Archangel Gabriel

Dearest Archangel Gabriel, please allow your power and strength to guide me at this time and protect me from negative influences. With your help, I know this will be an exciting and positive time, free from stress and difficulties.

Meditation with Archangel Gabriel for Help in Making Major Changes

Prepare yourself by sitting in front of your altar, and lighting your candle. The flame represents the spark of the Divine within that gives you the courage and strength to adjust to this time of transition in your life. Perform the relaxation exercise as detailed in chapter 2. Say the prayer to Archangel Gabriel, and then imagine yourself in your inner temple. Know that your Guardian Angel is beside you to give you all the love and support you need.

Before you stands Archangel Gabriel in a beautiful radiant light of gold. Feel this light enfolding you in a comforting aura of love and protective power. Know that all will be well and that you will adjust to this major transition in your life with the greatest of ease. Archangel Gabriel will protect you and support you through this time. Hold yourself in the golden light of the archangel and feel his loving power permeating every cell of your being. All is well in your life, and changes will be completed without any problems or stress.

Hold this feeling for as long as you feel comfortable, then bring yourself back to your actual surroundings. Close your chakras as detailed in chapter 2, and take a sip of water. It is best to do this meditation at least once a week until you feel you are through the change and you have adjusted to your new way of life.

The love and power of Archangel Gabriel will guide you to a positive and successful way of living and bring you great happiness and satisfaction. Life will feel worthwhile and exciting, and the angels will bring you the fulfillment of your dearest dreams.

Chapter 23
ARCHANGEL GABRIEL:
HEALING ANXIETY

Anxiety is a very debilitating illness and is closely linked to depression. Like depression, anxiety seriously affects your life and stops you from doing many of the things that gave you pleasure and joy. Anxiety affects all areas of your life and can come upon you for varying reasons. It is very difficult to get rid of once it has got a grip on you. It can make everyday tasks difficult to perform, as the fear grips your stomach and makes even the simplest of tasks a major effort.

Depression is greatly healed by Archangel Jophiel, as detailed in chapter 28, and Archangel Gabriel can bring the strength of the Divine to help ease the crippling hold of anxiety. If you suffer from anxiety, you should always seek medical advice, for there is a range of prescription drugs available that can greatly help the condition.

The healing of Archangel Gabriel goes hand in hand with medication to bring a resolution to the problem, which seems to take over your life. Just getting through the day is an effort, but the healing light of Gabriel will break through the darkness that has you in its grip and bring gentle healing. With anxiety, instead of embracing the challenge of each new day, you feel unable to cope with anything and the day becomes a struggle to get through. The purpose of the day becomes not "What can I achieve?" but "How can I get through it?" This is a situation that doesn't help anyone and can place great stress on your relationships.

Anxiety is an all-consuming illness that is very difficult to break out of without help. Once it has you in its grip, the smallest problem can grow totally out of proportion and create more anxiety. Anxiety feeds on anxiety, but the power of Archangel Gabriel will give you the strength to break out of its grip and give you the courage to face your tasks and problems. When suffering from anxiety, those things that once gave you excitement and pleasure no longer do so. Indeed, the thought of doing such things creates its own anxiety, but Archangel Gabriel can heal these negative feelings and return to you the pleasure you once enjoyed. Archangel Gabriel's power is the strength of the Divine and can heal and put in perspective all your problems that cause anxiety. Meditation with Gabriel will bring his deep wisdom to your soul and you will be able to see ways around your problems, thereby healing the anxiety such problems cause.

When in the grip of anxiety, you often visualize the future filled with unimaginable horrors, with all your worst fears coming true. But you cannot know what the future will bring. Focusing on one day at a time will help bring such thoughts under control, and with the help of Archangel Gabriel and your Guardian Angel you will be able to turn these fears around and look forward to an exciting future. Your future depends on your thoughts and actions in the present moment, so it is important to keep your thoughts healthy and positive.

The love and light of Gabriel will bring healing to your thoughts and fears and bring the realization that the future does not have to be as you imagine. You can do something positive about it with Gabriel's help. The angels will never let you down but will see you through difficult situations to a positive conclusion. Never fear, for with angels by your side, all will be well in your life. The angels are with you always, looking after you and helping to steer you along a positive and happy route. Your worst nightmares have no basis in reality, for they are only figments of your imagination, and with angels by your side, you have nothing to fear. You are cherished and loved by an almighty power that has the ability to bring positivity out of whatever negative conditions you currently find yourself in.

Finding the cause for your anxiety is of great help, for if you know the cause, you are halfway there to healing the situation. Money is a major concern for many people, and money problems can lead to great stress on the nervous system. By bringing the healing power of Gabriel into your life, you will find the inspiration and courage to take whatever steps are necessary to resolve the problems you face. It is truly amazing what can happen when Archangel Gabriel brings his healing power to your life. Miracles do indeed happen!

The meditation with Gabriel in this chapter will bring upliftment from the crippling anxiety that blocks inspiration and joy from being a part of your life. Once the anxiety is under control, the way is clear for a more positive outlook, which will bring its own healing to enable you to take positive action and once more lead a fulfilling and joyful life.

Gabriel's healing of anxiety is truly magical. He is a bringer of inspiration and joy, and you will find that all those things that gave you pleasure in the past now do so again. Angelic healing will help you live a truly inspirational life, with the power and love of Gabriel always by your side. While you need him, he will never leave you but will always be there to bring upliftment and hope and the knowledge that all will be well in your life. Archangel Gabriel knows the suffering anxiety brings and does not stand in judgment of you in any way whatsoever. His only purpose is to heal and restore happiness to the depleted soul, and this he does in the most miraculous ways.

You can feel very alone when suffering from extreme anxiety, for it is a difficult condition to talk about with anyone. Those who don't suffer from it do not understand how debilitating an illness it is. But Archangel Gabriel does understand and knows that it is something you cannot just shake yourself out of. It is good to know that right by your side is this angel who completely understands your plight and brings his love to you as a healing balm upon your illness. Healing will take place when you actively join with

Gabriel in meditation to heal and uplift your soul. The healing of Gabriel will be manifold, for he will heal deeply into your soul, where the seed of the illness lies. He will also heal your mental body, where thoughts of a negative nature go round and round, feeding the anxiety. His loving touch will also heal your emotional body, which holds all the fear associated with anxiety, and he will bring you the courage and strength to face up to things and gain insight and inspiration into how to deal with them.

Miracles occur when you actively seek the healing of angels, and Gabriel will bring magic and miracles to your life that will once again bring joy and happiness to your soul. Practice the following meditation with Gabriel on a daily basis and gradually the anxiety will fade and a new positive outlook will take its place. You will know that the future holds only inspiration and joy, for nothing can go wrong when you have angel love to uphold you.

PRAYER TO ARCHANGEL GABRIEL

Dearest Archangel Gabriel, I thank you for your healing power that comes to me as I struggle with anxiety. Your love and inspiration uplift me and lead me through the darkness to a joyous and fulfilling life.

MEDITATION WITH ARCHANGEL GABRIEL TO HEAL ANXIETY

Sit before your angel altar with your back straight, and make sure you are warm and comfortable. Light your candle to remind yourself of the light that shines within you that is the spark of the Divine. Say the prayer to Archangel Gabriel to focus your mind on the work you are about to do. Take a few deep breaths to calm yourself, then do the relaxation exercise as detailed in chapter 2. When fully relaxed, imagine yourself in your inner temple. Take a few moments to look around and fully imagine yourself there. Your Guardian Angel welcomes you with outstretched arms and envelops you in a beautiful golden light. He or she stands behind you with hands resting on your shoulders to give you support during the meditation.

See standing before you a magnificent angel bathed in a soft golden light. This is the Archangel Gabriel, who gives you all his love. Feel the light radiating from Gabriel and enveloping you in its power. Feel this wonderful light calming your fears and anxieties and replacing such negative feelings with joy and courage. Know that all will be well in your life and nothing can go wrong, for you are looked after by angels twenty-four hours a day. You feel a great surge of happiness at this realization that floods your whole being—

mind, body, and soul—and brings a profound healing to your battered emotions. Gabriel continues to flood you with his golden light, a light that heals and uplifts and brings inspiration. You know that each day henceforth will be a day of happiness and courage and that your anxiety and fears will melt away in the light of Gabriel.

Hold yourself in the golden light of Gabriel for as long as you feel comfortable, then bring your awareness back to your actual surroundings. Give thanks to Gabriel for his healing of your mind, body, and soul. Take a few deep breaths, then close down your chakras as detailed in chapter 2. Take a few sips of water to further ground yourself, and don't forget to snuff out your candle!

The healing of Gabriel will continue long after the meditation has ended, and each day you will feel a little more confident, a little more at peace with yourself and your life. Practice this meditation daily until you feel that your anxieties and fears are a thing of the past and that a full healing has taken place. It is a relief to feel strong about the future instead of fearing what it will bring. You now feel happy and able to face all of life's challenges with a joyful heart, knowing that the Archangel Gabriel will never desert you, but will always be there for you with his love and healing.

Chapter 24
ARCHANGEL CHAMUEL:
HELP ON THE SPIRITUAL PATH

Maybe you have come to a point in your life where you are looking for meaning above and beyond the materialistic world of everyday living. There are many routes to finding the divine spark within you and many ways to work with the Divine. It can be difficult to know which one is right, but you should always follow your heart and do what feels right for you. Once on the spiritual path, there are many distractions and many misleading side roads you can go down, for the ego will feel under threat, but working with angels will always guide you along a beautiful and true pathway that is right for you. All people are different and have different needs, and that includes spiritual needs. "All roads lead to

God" is something to be remembered, which makes religious intolerance so absurd.

The spiritual quest can be confusing at times, but Archangel Chamuel will guide you through it to find the right answers to your questions and bring you to a place of knowing and deep peace. If you feel confused or are not sure about a particular spiritual path you are following, ask Chamuel for guidance by doing the simple meditation in this chapter. You will soon have answers to your questions, and confusion will be turned into a deep knowing that you are on the right path.

Finding the divine spark within is the sole purpose of our lives, and angels are ever by our side to help us in this quest. It is the search for the Holy Grail, and angels are our guides and helpers. Archangel Chamuel is by your side as soon as you purposefully seek spiritual enlightenment and search for that spark within. Chamuel will guide you and lead you to the path that best suits your needs, and he will always be by your side to whisper words of encouragement and inspiration. There often comes a time on the spiritual path when you feel confused as to whether you are doing the right thing or not. Archangel Chamuel will uplift you at such times and bring you an inner confidence and knowing that all is well and that you are on the right path, for you are guided by angels.

You may have many questions once you endeavor to follow a spiritual path, and Chamuel will be there for you with answers. Always have a notebook and pen handy, for Chamuel can bring you answers at any time, sometimes when you least expect it. The following meditation will bring the wisdom of Chamuel to your heart and mind and bring answers where there is confusion and questions.

PRAYER TO ARCHANGEL CHAMUEL

Dearest Archangel Chamuel, you know that the spiritual path has many pitfalls. We ask for your love and guidance as we continue our journey and pray that we have your wisdom to guide us. We thank you for this guidance and know that your love clears our vision as we walk our chosen path.

MEDITATION WITH ARCHANGEL CHAMUEL FOR SPIRITUAL HELP

This is an important meditation, for it will give you clearer vision and bring many insights and answers to questions you may have about your spiritual path. Chamuel guides all those who make the determined effort to seek spiritual enlightenment, and his love and wisdom will guide you every day of your life.

Sit comfortably, either in a chair or on the floor, with your back straight. Have your altar in front of you, and light your candle. Focus on the flame for a few moments, remembering that it symbolizes the flame of the Divine at your heart center. The aim of this meditation is for this little spark to grow and flood your whole life and being with divine love and wisdom.

Relax yourself as detailed in chapter 2, then say the prayer to Archangel Chamuel. Imagine yourself in your temple with your Guardian Angel beside you to help and inspire you. Before you stands Archangel Chamuel in a glorious white light. Hold this image and feel the light flooding your whole being. There is no need to think of anything; just hold yourself in the beautiful light and know that divine guidance will ensure that your questions will be answered. The pure white light of Archangel Chamuel makes you feel very happy and uplifted because you know that you are on the right path, which leads to fulfillment and enlightenment.

When you feel ready, bring your attention back to your actual surroundings and give thanks to Archangel Chamuel for his help and guidance. Close down your chakras as detailed in chapter 2, and take a sip of water to further ground yourself. Over the next few days, you will receive many insights and answers to problems that have been troubling you. If you have felt doubts about which path to follow, these doubts will be clarified and you will feel a newfound confidence in the path you have chosen.

Chapter 25

ARCHANGEL CHAMUEL:
ATTRACTING ABUNDANCE
AND PROSPERITY

One of the biggest areas of confusion on the spiritual path is the question of prosperity and money. It is one of the most emotional issues and can cause the most distress. Many people cannot equate spirituality with being rich and prosperous, and cause themselves a lot of heartache and hardship trying to reconcile the two. Being rich and prosperous is often seen as something unspiritual and a hindrance to the spiritual life. These beliefs can cause a lack in one's life.

Angels are only too willing to help with financial problems, and working with them can bring abundance and prosperity into your life. Archangel Chamuel in particular will help with confusion and misconceptions about prosperity. The state of your finances will depend on your beliefs about money. If you feel you don't deserve to be prosperous for some reason or that you cannot have money because you wish to be a "spiritual" person, you are going to live a life of lack.

I know this feeling very well indeed. I have had great difficulty following a "spiritual" life and reconciling the need for money. I have created lack in my life, and it is only with the help of angels bringing me to a place of understanding that I have been able to provide for myself properly. Everyone has the right to a secure roof over their head, enough food to eat, clothing to keep warm, and enough money to provide heating and comfort when necessary. Don't forget that those folks who follow the spiritual path as nuns or monks have all their material needs met for them, including a secure dwelling place and food and clothing. They may have given up the materialistic life and withdrawn from the world, but their needs are still being met for them.

There is nothing wrong with enjoying all the beautiful things the world has to offer and being prosperous. But if you are jealous of extreme wealth or covet other people's good fortune and possessions, you will need the help of the angels to bring you peace and acceptance. Money in itself is not evil, but it is the greed for money and the willingness to do anything to get it that is so damaging to the soul. Wealthy people are not sinful in any way, but if you judge them as unspiritual, you are most unlikely to ever be wealthy yourself. Wealthy people can be very spiritual people doing wonderful things with their wealth. We all have the right to the good things in life, but guilt can arise when we think of all the people in the world who live in extreme poverty. No one should feel guilty about being wealthy. The world is abundant, and it is the wish of the angels for all of us to be prosperous.

If you have a problem with money, you need to dissolve the beliefs at their root cause and find out where these beliefs come from. Maybe your parents were poor and you were brought up in an atmosphere of lack, in which case you may well believe that you do not deserve to be prosperous. If your parents were envious of rich people, you may well believe that to be prosperous is somehow evil and not a road you wish to go down. You may not realize that you have these beliefs, for they will be buried deep within you and not immediately obvious and it will take quite a bit of work to truly dissolve them. This is where Archangel Chamuel can be so helpful, for his power can resolve these issues easily and lead you to a path of prosperity and abundance. The meditation with him in this chapter will help heal these negative beliefs and bring you the prosperity you so richly deserve and are entitled to as a child of the universe.

Being wealthy does not necessarily mean having a lot of money. One can have abundance in many ways. A life rich in happiness and fulfillment is an abundant life. If you have lots of friends and a supportive family, you are indeed rich in many ways. Often we want more than we actually have and do not appreciate what we do have. Archangel Chamuel will help heal these misconceptions and bring a deep peace to the soul and an appreciation of the richness in our lives.

PRAYER TO ARCHANGEL CHAMUEL

Dearest Archangel Chamuel, help us to understand that the world is an abundant and prosperous place and a lack of any kind is not in the divine plan for us. Lift the veil of confusion from our eyes and help us enjoy all the abundance and riches that the world has to offer.

Meditation with Archangel Chamuel for Abundance and Prosperity

Sit comfortably in front of your altar, and light the candle flame as a reminder of the little spark of the Divine within. Make sure that your back is straight and that you are warm and comfortable. Say the prosperity prayer to Chamuel, then do the relaxation exercise as described in chapter 2. Imagine yourself in your temple, with your Guardian Angel beside you for help and support.

See standing before you the glorious Archangel Chamuel radiating a beautiful golden light that enfolds you and permeates your whole being. Know that prosperity and abundance are the right of all children of the universe, and know that from now on you are going to believe in a prosperous and abundant world. Know that you are entitled to your share of this abundance and that your wealth will increase a hundredfold. Feel Chamuel's glorious light penetrating deep into your soul, where negative beliefs lie unrecognized and are doing so much harm to your prosperity. Know that these negative beliefs are dissolved in the light of Archangel Chamuel and that all will be well from now on in your life. Prosperity and abundance will be yours and your life will be happier and more complete.

Hold this feeling in the golden light of Chamuel for as long as you feel comfortable, then bring your attention back to your actual surroundings. You feel greatly uplifted and happy and are no longer confused over the issue of money. You know that you can provide for yourself with the greatest of ease and that wealth will flow into your life. It is believing these things that is half the battle with the problem of poverty or lack. Do this meditation every day, and you will soon see a difference in your finances.

Try some positive affirmations as well, for these will aid your efforts to live a life of prosperity. Here are some possibilities:

The world is an abundant place,
and I deserve all the abundance the world has to offer.

I feel happy and comfortable being prosperous.

Abundance and prosperity come easily to me.

Chapter 26

ARCHANGEL JOPHIEL:
FINDING CREATIVE INSPIRATION

When you are lacking creative inspiration, life can feel rather dull. Beauty is an important ingredient that can lift your spirits and add a new dimension to life. You may feel that there is no beauty in your life and that where you live is not a beautiful place, but there is much natural beauty around if you look for it. You can have flowering plants indoors to bring a touch of beauty to your surroundings. The sky is always beautiful if you take the time to look at it.

You may feel your surroundings are not attractive in any way, but you can do much to make them inspirational. Surround yourself with beauty in any form. Take photographs of things that appeal to you, or cut out pictures from magazines that you find beautiful and inspiring and pin them up someplace where you can see them often. If you have some money to spare, treat yourself to bunches of flowers or buy beautiful textiles to brighten up your home.

Everyone should experience some kind of beauty and creativity in their life. If this is not so for you, then Archangel Jophiel is the angel to tune in to, as he is the angel of art and beauty. Meditation with Jophiel will bring inspiration to your heart and mind, whether you are a creative person suffering from a block or someone wishing to explore latent creative talents.

Let your talents shine! Archangel Jophiel will help you realize your latent talents and take you on a journey of self-discovery. Perhaps you have always wanted to do a particular thing but have never had the confidence to develop it. Meditation with Archangel Jophiel will help you find the confidence and bring to you a deeper knowledge of yourself. By finding the beauty that is within, you can create that beauty in your surroundings. Archangel Jophiel will help you to find the determination and ability to pursue your chosen hobby and dreams, and with the help of angels, who knows where that will lead!

Perhaps you don't know what your latent talents are, in which case meditation with Archangel Jophiel will bring a deeper understanding and knowledge of yourself and draw out that which is latent within you. Inspiration will come. Perhaps when you were a child you loved doing something but now do not have time to follow such pursuits or lack the confidence to pursue them. Archangel Jophiel will bring ideas to your mind and confidence to your heart.

Perhaps when you were a child you had an exciting hobby that engrossed you, be it a sport, singing, music, painting, or needlework. The list is endless, but development of unfulfilled dreams can have a healing effect on all aspects of your life and make you a more rounded person.

Fulfillment of latent talents can help you solve various problems in your life, for you will feel more satisfied, and indeed life might become exciting, bringing a new contentment to your days. Such fulfillment can bring a healing to your life where there was negativity and also bring a new happiness and joy.

Meditation with Archangel Jophiel will bring a heightened awareness of the beauty around you in the world, which in itself will also bring a new joy and happiness to your life. By meditating with Archangel Jophiel, you will be touching the very core of your being, your inner spirit, which is beautiful beyond words, and by doing this on a regular basis, the beauty of your spirit will begin to manifest in your daily life. This can bring surprises, for when you work with the inner spirit, very positive things can happen.

The creation of beautiful things has its own rewards and can create harmony in your life in many different ways. Meditation with Archangel Jophiel will allow your inner beauty to flourish, for it is not outer beauty that really matters as much as inner beauty, which meditation with Archangel Jophiel will bring forth. When this inner beauty is allowed to color your life, you will feel yourself changing in many positive ways. A new realization will come to you about how to live your life in a more harmonious way.

Dwelling on the negative aspects of life can damage the soul and bring about a negative viewpoint, thereby attracting negative things to you, but by focusing on the beauty within, life itself will automatically take on a beautiful, thoughtful, and more positive aspect. You will become aware of those parts of your nature that are perhaps not so beautiful, but the power of Archangel Jophiel can bring a clarity of vision to correct such negativity and replace it with positive thoughts and actions.

You can make beautiful things instead of buying them. They will have so much more value if they are home-made. Appreciating all the beauty in nature that surrounds you every day will bring great joy to the soul. Even if you live in a city, there are parks and trees and gardens that give great pleasure. Enjoy these things and refresh your soul by tuning in to nature. It will bring beauty and harmony to your soul, which will manifest in your life. Something as simple as smiling can have a profound effect on the soul, and who knows, someone might smile back!

Archangel Jophiel will nourish the inner beauty of your spirit and bring great joy and happiness to your everyday living. Practice of the meditation with Archangel Jophiel in this chapter will bring great rewards, for we all have inner beauty and talents that we can contribute to the world.

Practice this meditation on a daily basis and you will feel wonderful changes taking place within you. Your life will take on a new purpose as Jophiel reveals to you latent talents and gifts that you can develop to create a more contented and beautiful life for yourself.

Archangel Jophiel has the power to see deep into your soul and to see the real beauty of your being. Regular meditation with him will manifest this beauty and bring it into your everyday life, enabling you to live a much happier life that is worthwhile and beneficial not only to yourself but to all those you know. Your relationships will become that much easier and happier as you bring the beauty of Jophiel to bear in your dealings with others. Spreading happiness and beauty is one of the most important things you can do, and you can bring the benefit of Jophiel's love to bear not only in your own life but in the lives of others.

Prayer to Archangel Jophiel

Dearest Archangel Jophiel, reveal to me the beauty of my true being and help me discover the gifts of the Divine that I can use in my everyday life. Let me see beauty around me and help me appreciate that which is positive and worthwhile.

Meditation with Archangel Jophiel for Creative Inspiration

Sit comfortably either on the floor or in a chair, with your back straight, before your angel altar. Light your candle to remind yourself of the spark of the Divine within. Say the prayer to Jophiel to focus your mind on what you wish to achieve, then do the relaxation exercise as detailed in chapter 2. Imagine yourself in your inner temple, where your Guardian Angel awaits you with outstretched arms and enfolds you in a golden ray of love. He or she stands behind you with hands resting on your shoulders in support.

Imagine before you a beautiful and magnificent angel bathed in rose-colored light. Feel this light permeating your entire being so that your body, mind, and soul are flooded with this beautiful rose light. Feel the light healing where there is negativity. Know also that it is working on your inner being to discover your latent talents and the natural beauty of your spirit and bring them to your outer consciousness. Bathe yourself in this light for as long as you feel comfortable, and know that it brings happiness and inspiration and a great beauty to your life.

When you feel ready, bring your awareness back to your temple and then to your actual surroundings. Take a few deep breaths and close your chakras as detailed in chapter 2 to really ground yourself. Take a few sips of water if you wish, and don't forget to put out your candle!

Be prepared to get some really great ideas and inspirations over the next few days. The more you practice this meditation, the more real beauty you will see in your life. Have the courage to act on any ideas that come to you, for they may be life-changing.

Chapter 27

ARCHANGEL JOPHIEL:
HEALING DEPRESSION

Depression is a very serious illness that should never go unchecked, for it affects not only yourself but all those around you. Archangel Jophiel will bring his great love to heal your soul if you feel depressed or down about something, and regular meditation with him will lift your spirits out of the darkness and bring joy to your heart once again.

Archangel Jophiel can bring relief from serious depression, for he is able to penetrate the thick black blanket of depression that seems to envelop you when it really gets a hold. He can bring the warmth and vigor of the sun to dispel those dark clouds and dissolve the blackness you feel you are drowning in.

Depression is a very debilitating illness and can affect all areas of your life. It can affect your work by interfering with your power to concentrate and communicate, and can also have a damaging effect on relationships. Sometimes when you are feeling depressed you just don't want to relate to anyone else. All the joy of living has gone from you, and you feel unable to perform even the simplest of tasks.

When depression comes upon you, it is difficult to have the enthusiasm to do anything, particularly meditation, but just imagining the joyous golden light of Archangel Jophiel enfolding you in loving understanding can have miraculous effects. If you suffer from deep depression, seek medical advice, for there are many prescription drugs available that can really help the condition. If you don't wish to take antidepressants, it may be beneficial to practice the meditation with Jophiel in this chapter when you are feeling up to it. If you imagine yourself wrapped in golden light, this will work on the disharmony within that is causing the depression.

Meditation may just be too much of an effort when you are in a deeply depressive mood, but just imagining yourself wrapped in the warm golden light of Archangel Jophiel will help lift that black cloud. Imagine the light as glorious sunshine permeating every part of your being. The power of Jophiel will radiate deep into your soul, where the seeds of the depression lie, and the powerful light will bring healing and a new enthusiasm to live life to the full.

As a sufferer of depression, I can vouch for the uplifting effect of the light of Jophiel, for it really does break through that thick dark cloud that seems to envelop you when you sink into depression. I have found that I cannot practice meditation at such times, but just trying to make the effort to imagine the golden light of Jophiel radiating throughout my whole being, body and soul, does have a very healing effect. It opens the way for true healing to take place, which can be done through meditation with Archangel Jophiel, for his strong golden light can shine on the darkest of places within the soul and transform the darkness into light and joy.

It is worthwhile to remember that when the black cloud sinks upon you, the angels do not abandon you. Indeed, they are with you in force to help uplift and heal you and bring their joyous message of love to bear upon your soul. You may not be aware of angel presence when you are in the clutches of the darkness, but Archangel Jophiel is beside you, as is your Guardian Angel, and they are both working to lift the cloud of depression and bring joy and enthusiasm back to your life.

Depression can come about due to bereavement or the loss of a job, and these are very difficult situations to deal with. But the love of the angels is always with you to bring acceptance, hope, and optimism for the future. Know that the angels are always by your side whispering words of encouragement. However difficult the situation you find yourself in, know that the love of the angels is there to help and guide you. Working with your Guardian Angel can also be really helpful and rewarding when faced with a difficult problem.

Depression is an illness that can affect anyone at any time for no apparent reason. But often there is an underlying problem that causes the depression. The power of Jophiel can uncover the causes of the depression, and this in itself can be very healing, for you then have the opportunity to heal the root of your illness. Working with Archangel Jophiel every day will bring enlightenment as to why you feel as you do, and he will bring all his love and wisdom to bear upon the problem. Jophiel will bring all his power and love to you if you seriously try to heal this root cause, and it can be done safely and powerfully in the knowledge that the angel's healing power is uplifting you and protecting you from negative sources. Seeing the cause of depression clearly will weaken the hold it has on you, and having Jophiel's support will bring healing ever closer. Archangel Jophiel will be with you as you look at the causes of your depression, and he will help you deal with the problem.

It may be helpful to write out a description of the causes of your depression and work out some positive affirmations to counteract them. Writing down the causes can be very cathartic, as this process is in effect getting the problem out of your system. Letting go of the root causes of depression can be a very great help. Say to yourself, "I let go of all negative influences in my life." Working with Archangel Jophiel will help you look at your life with a greater understanding, and his love will support you and help you work through your demons. Remember that we are all very powerful beings with powerful minds that, when guided by angels, can heal even the deepest depression.

Keep a depression diary and make a note of how you are feeling from day to day. The healing of Archangel Jophiel is very powerful, and you should notice a difference quite soon. Practice the meditation every day if you can, and you will soon find that you once more feel joy and enthusiasm for your daily tasks. The pessimistic outlook on life will be transformed into a new and exciting optimism for the future, and you will experience the attacks of the dark clouds less and less.

PRAYER TO ARCHANGEL JOPHIEL

Dearest Archangel Jophiel, I pray that your healing light will shine on the darkness within me and transform that darkness into light so that depressive moods cannot take hold of me. I thank you for your healing power to lift me above the dark clouds that limit my life. Your beautiful light brings me to a place of healing and joy where darkness has been banished.

MEDITATION WITH ARCHANGEL JOPHIEL TO HEAL DEPRESSION

Sit comfortably before your altar and light your candle. Concentrate on the flame for a while, and remind yourself that it represents the flame of God within your spirit. That little flame within has a very healing effect when activated and can banish depression and sadness. Take a few deep breaths, and then do the relaxation exercise as detailed in chapter 2. Say the prayer to Archangel Jophiel, then imagine yourself in your inner temple with your Guardian Angel beside you to give love and support. You feel very safe and happy in your inner temple, and your Guardian Angel bathes you in a golden light to help you with your work with the Archangel Jophiel.

See before you a beautiful golden angel radiating a bright golden light. This light fills your whole temple with sunshine and enfolds you in a lovely warm and calm feeling. You feel that all is well with your life. Feel this golden light radiating throughout your whole being—physical, mental, and spiritual. Feel this light penetrating to the darkest areas of your soul where the depression lies, and feel it healing you. Know that the illness will be diminished and eventually healed by the golden light of Jophiel. Hold yourself in the glorious golden light of Jophiel for as long as you feel comfortable. You feel very safe and uplifted by this glorious light and know that a wonderful healing is taking place.

When you feel ready, bring your awareness back to your actual surroundings and take a few deep breaths. Close down your chakras as detailed in chapter 2, and take a few sips of water to properly ground yourself. Give thanks to Archangel Jophiel for his healing power, and know that this power will continue to heal and uplift you long after your meditation is finished. Don't forget to put out your candle.

Know that all will be well and that the golden light of Jophiel will reveal to you the causes of the depression you suffer. Know that he will give to you the courage and ability to safely deal with this and bring healing where there is darkness in your soul.

You should always seek medical advice about depression. If you have been prescribed medication, do not give this up when practicing the meditation with Jophiel. The work you do with Jophiel will bring about a wonderful healing, and if you feel you can now live without medication, this should be done gradually under medical supervision. I speak from experience and know that my own healing was brought about by the wonderful loving help of this beautiful angel and also with the help of my Guardian Angel working with Jophiel.

Have confidence in the healing of the angels, for it really does work, and know that the dark clouds can be lifted and vanquished by the light of angels. Enjoyment of life will return, and the dark clouds will descend less and less as you persevere with this meditation. Perform the meditation every day at the same time for maximum benefit.

Chapter 28

ARCHANGEL RAGUEL:
GAINING SELF-CONFIDENCE

Holding back from life can have a very detrimental effect on your development and progress and lead you to miss golden opportunities that could create wonderful successes and achievements. Lack of self-confidence is an ego issue, for it is the ego that lacks the confidence to take hold of life with a confident and happy heart. The spirit deep within has all the confidence you need to lead a full and glorious life, but fear is at the root of a lack of self-confidence and you need to understand what you are actually afraid of. It can be fear of making a fool of yourself or, more commonly, fear of failure that triggers the negative feelings of lack of confidence.

When you are working from the spirit within, fear is abolished, for the spirit knows you have the power to achieve all you wish to achieve. The spirit can guide you to tackle difficult issues and take opportunities as they present themselves. The spirit understands that failure does not mean making a fool of yourself and that failure is not the end of opportunity. So-called failure means that something was not right for you at a particular time, and there is no harm at all in trying again at a later date. Archangel Raguel will connect you to your inner spirit and enfold you in love and healing, which will bring confidence to your heart and mind.

Meditation with Archangel Raguel will bring the knowledge that all is well with your life and that you do have the courage to overcome any failures that occur. Practicing the meditation with Raguel will bring a newfound confidence to your heart, the kind of confidence that can only come from the Divine.

When setting out on a new course of action, there is always the nagging doubt that it will result in failure. But you can never know at the beginning if your efforts will fail. Why should they? More than likely you will be successful, and with the help of the angels this is very likely to be the case. Your own dear Guardian Angel will be with you as you tackle life's challenges to help you through and bring you to a place of happiness and success. Sometimes things work out differently from what you expected; this should never be seen as failure but rather as another golden opportunity that can take you in an exciting direction you had not anticipated.

Shying away from challenges will get you nowhere, but Archangel Raguel will always be by your side if you ask for his help to bring you the confidence you need as you face up to life and take on challenges as they appear. Raguel will bring a peace to your heart and a sense of well-being with the knowledge that all is well in your life. Nothing can go drastically wrong if you have the courage to face up to mistakes without fear and with the joyful knowledge that so-called mistakes are simply lessons to be happily learned before moving on.

No one likes failure, and it can lead to feelings of inadequacy and depression, but the power of Archangel Raguel will lift your spirits from these negative feelings and bring a renewed hope to your being that will encourage you to take on your tasks with a fresh enthusiasm and lack of fear.

The person who experiences a lack of confidence expects every action and decision to fail, and this breeds a very negative attitude toward life that attracts negativity. If you expect to fail, then it is very likely that you will fail, for you will not be putting your whole heart and spirit into the task. There may be a deep-rooted reason for these negative beliefs. Maybe you were brought up to look at life in a negative way and believe that good things do not happen to you but only to other people who are more worthy. These are destructive feelings and are corrosive to your life, but the Archangel Raguel can bring his light of understanding to shine on these beliefs and let you see them for what they are—just negative beliefs that have no basis in reality. Archangel Raguel will heal this negativity that is deep within your soul and enfold you in his healing light to bring you a new happiness and the knowledge that things *can* go right for you and that you have as much right as anyone else to achieve your goals and have happy experiences.

Archangel Raguel brings healing love to the frightened soul and enables you to view life with a positive outlook. He brings healing deep into your soul where negativity lies and brings a sense of well-being and joy that enables you to do things you never thought possible! When you accept Archangel Raguel's healing, your life will take on a new and happier course that you never thought possible.

Feelings of self-doubt will diminish daily when you practice the meditation with Raguel in this chapter, and these negative feelings will be replaced with feelings of confidence and joy that will bring exciting experiences to your life. Courage will replace fear and lack of confidence, and new inspiration and hope will fill your life. You will have the confidence to see setbacks for what they are—simply setbacks and not the end of the world.

Meditation with Archangel Raguel will help develop the divine spark of God within that does not know failure and can only bring a joyous success to everything you do. When working from the divine spark within, you will always succeed, for the divine spark brings divine power to all your efforts. Success is guaranteed when working with angels, and confidence will grow daily as you practice the meditation and work more and more from the ever-brightening spark of the Divine within.

Never fear that failure is the end of all your dreams, for Raguel will reveal to you the joy of positive hope and bring to you the knowledge that you *will* get where you want to be with the wondrous help of angels. Newfound confidence will flood your being and happiness will fill your days when working with angels. Lack of self-confidence will become a thing of the past, and your life will take on a new momentum and meaning that you never thought possible.

The belief that you are not good enough will be replaced with the knowledge that you *are* good enough and are capable of achieving your most precious dreams.

Lack of confidence often makes you unable to speak up for yourself when in the company of others, and this can seriously blight your relationships. Perhaps your lack of confidence makes it difficult to make friends, but the meditation with Archangel Raguel will bring a new confidence to this negative condition. Lack of friends often stems again from fear—the fear of being hurt—and this is again a fault in the ego. You will find that your relationships and friendships flourish when you have the confidence in yourself to join in conversations and contribute your own unique viewpoint.

Practice the meditation with Archangel Raguel daily to bring this newfound confidence to your heart and make your life a happy adventure free of fear and failure. The meditation works on the ego, which is afraid of failure and hurts, and it unites you with your inner being that knows all is well and that you do have the ability to speak up for yourself and achieve your dreams.

Your lack of confidence may well be a result of low self-esteem, and the Archangel Raguel can help you overcome such a debilitating belief. Low self-esteem lies in a mistaken belief of the ego that you are not worthy or important. The spirit within knows that you are a magnificent and beautiful being and that you have the great love of the angels. Every individual is important in the eyes of the angels and in the eyes of God or you would not be here. All of us have some part to play in the grand scheme of things, and everyone has a unique contribution to make to the whole.

No one should have the belief that they are worthless, and the angels are beside you with their love and encouragement to bring you to the belief that you *are* worthy and that you *are* a unique human being. We are all unique in a very special way, and the love of the angels will bring out this uniqueness and bring healing to your life. To the angels, you are very important indeed, for you help bring their healing power to the world.

Low self-esteem usually stems from childhood experiences where you were in some way made to feel worthless or unimportant. Archangel Raguel brings you the truth that we are all important in our own way and that no one on earth is unworthy. Archangel Raguel brings healing to your soul with the belief that you are a magnificent spiritual being. Self-confidence and good self-esteem are the natural states of your being, and when these are restored by the angels, you will be able to live life to the full in a joyous and worthwhile manner.

Prayer to Archangel Raguel

Dearest Archangel Raguel, I give thanks for your help in overcoming lack of confidence in my life and know that your wondrous power and love are always there for me whenever I need them. I pray and give thanks that you are able to take away my fears and help me build a happy and inspirational life.

Meditation with Archangel Raguel for Self-Confidence

Sit comfortably before your angel altar, either on the floor or in a chair. Light a candle on your altar to remind yourself of the little light that shines within that is part of the divine power. Say the prayer to Archangel Raguel and take a few deep breaths to calm yourself before doing the relaxation exercise as detailed in chapter 2. Imagine yourself in your inner temple, where your Guardian Angel greets you with outstretched arms and enfolds you in a glorious golden light. You feel safe and secure in your inner temple and know that the meditation with Archangel Raguel will bring happiness and achievement to your life.

Imagine standing in front of you a magnificent angel clothed in golden robes and radiating a beautiful golden light. This light envelops you in a warm glow and uplifts you with a feeling of safety and joy. Feel the light from Archangel Raguel penetrating deep into your soul where fear and lack of confidence lie, and know that the light is gradually melting these feelings away, leaving you happy and self-confident about your life. Archangel Raguel brings you the truth that you are good enough and that you have great abilities and the power to accomplish all you set out to do. Fear and lack of confidence are things of the past, and with Archangel Raguel by your side, you can accomplish great things and make all your dreams come true. You feel very calm and happy bathed in the golden light of Raguel.

Hold yourself in this light for as long as you feel comfortable, and then bring your awareness back to your actual surroundings. Give thanks to Archangel Raguel for his work and his love for you. Take a few deep breaths, then close down your chakras as detailed in chapter 2. Take a few sips of water to further ground yourself, and don't forget to snuff out your candle!

Whenever fear or lack of confidence returns, just imagine Archangel Raguel by your side and you will feel a surge of confidence that you are capable of great achievements. Your Guardian Angel, too, is always with you to give you that extra bit of confidence when you need it and will help you through difficult times. You have the courage now to communicate fully with people where in the past you would hold back. You have the confidence to engage socially, and your relationships and friendships flourish. One of the worst aspects of a lack of confidence is that it can cut you off from other people and limit friendships. With the help of Archangel Raguel, you can now enjoy good relationships and banish loneliness and feelings of isolation forever.

The following affirmations may well be an extra help in your fight against lack of self-confidence and low self-esteem:

I am worthy and live my life to the full.

I have confidence in my abilities.

I am a unique and worthwhile person.

I give immeasurable help to the angels,
who appreciate my unique abilities.

Know that lack of confidence is a thing of the past. You can now move forward with all the confidence needed to develop your true potential and live a rewarding and joyous life.

Chapter 29

ANGELS:

SEEKING INDIVIDUAL HELP AND
SENDING LOVE INTO THE WORLD

Angels of the ninth choir are known simply as angels and include our Guardian Angels, who are with us all our lives. Angels are also very closely associated with nature, and it is these angels who look after and encourage the flowering and growing of individual plants and trees. They work closely with the Virtue angels in this respect.

Angels offer protection and advice and are very much concerned with matters that affect individual human beings. If you have had an "angel experience," it was probably one of these angels who came to you.

Angels work ceaselessly to bring the love of the Divine to the hearts of all humankind. Love is the greatest healer, and the angels have the deepest love for all humankind regardless of religion or whether someone is good or "bad." Sending angel love into the world is the most satisfying work you can do. When you tune in to these angels, you feel a great love and compassion for the whole of humankind and creation. When you experience the true love of the Divine in your heart, you feel the desire to send this love into the world where it is so badly needed to help those in distress through whatever conditions they are experiencing in life. Love heals the damaged hearts and minds of humankind. Love is the most potent of healers and can bring great comfort to people who are in despair, shattered by conflicts, homeless, bereaved, weary, or sorrowful.

The love of the angels will bring hope to those who feel hopeless and in despair, newfound energy and enthusiasm to those who feel weary, and inspiration and healing to those who feel down and depressed.

This love of the angels is very powerful and can work miracles in lives that are torn apart by negative influences. This may seem like ineffective work, for so many in the world need this help of the angels, but your work with the angels will heal someone somewhere.

If you are feeling down, in despair, or hopeless, then the meditation with the angels in this chapter will bring a new vitality to your life and awaken inspiration and love within your heart to lead a fulfilling and exciting life.

When you think of the cruelty and injustice in the world, it may seem like futile work to send out angel love, but the work of angels is never futile and always wins out in the end, however long it takes.

When sending out the love and light of the angels, never think of a particular person or group of people. Always just concentrate on sending this great love into the world and the angels will do the rest, for they will know where it is needed most.

Rest assured that someone, somewhere, will be touched by angels and be uplifted. The work will be made so much more powerful by your work on the earth plane. Your work will never, ever be wasted, for angel work is powerful and always works for good somewhere.

The angels are the angels who most often appear to humankind and give their help. They often appear as ordinary people who give assistance in some way and disappear as quickly as they appeared. It is not until they have gone that you are left wondering who they were and the realization dawns on you that they were angels.

Angels are the ones who give their help on an everyday basis to help us through the minor problems and tribulations of our lives. Nothing is too small for an angel to help you with, and they work closely with your Guardian Angel to bring you healing, inspiration, and upliftment. Call on the angels when you are in need of help for whatever reason, and you will feel the soft touch of angel wings to guide you along a positive path. Angels will also bring you messages, so always be open to thoughts and ideas that pop into your mind. If they are positive and give you a good feeling, they more than likely came from angels.

When working with angels to send love into the world, you are awakening the divine spark at the center of your being, and this can have a profound effect on your life. By sending out love, you attract love and positive elements to yourself, which can only make for a better and more rewarding life. Sending out the love of angels is the most satisfying work for the soul, and you will feel more fulfilled and inspired as you continue with this work. Practice the meditation in this chapter once a week if every day is too much, and know that you are making a great difference in the world. The pleasure you get from working with angels in this way will be life-changing for you, and the love you send out will be returned tenfold.

PRAYER TO THE ANGELS

Beloved angels, reveal to us your great love for all humankind and help us to nurture this love within ourselves. We give thanks that we can help you in your work of bringing the love of the Divine to all humankind to ease suffering and despair.

MEDITATION WITH THE ANGELS TO SEND THEIR LOVE INTO THE WORLD

Sit comfortably with your back straight, and light your candle. Focus on the flame for a few moments and remind yourself of the spark of divine love that dwells deep within you. Say the prayer to the angels to focus your mind on the work you are about to do. Perform the relaxation exercise detailed in chapter 2, then close your eyes and imagine yourself in your own special temple. Your Guardian Angel welcomes you with open arms and enfolds you in a lovely golden light. He or she stands behind you with hands resting on your shoulders to give you help and support during the meditation.

See before you a magnificent angel bathed in a rose-colored light, the light of love. Feel this light enfolding you and permeating every cell of your being. You feel uplifted and sharply focused on the special love of this angel. Feel yourself full of love for all humankind and send this love out into the world as a wonderful light that heals and uplifts where there is suffering, sorrow, and despair. By doing this work, you will be bringing light where there is darkness and helping the angels awaken the spark of the Divine that is in every one of us. Hold this feeling of sending love and light out into the world for as long as you feel comfortable.

If you are feeling particularly distressed, in despair, or just a bit down, feel this rose-colored light filling every cell of your being, bringing upliftment and healing. Know that you are never alone and that the angels are always by your side to bring hope and upliftment to your soul. Give thanks to the angels that you are able to share in their work of sending love into the world, and also give thanks for the healing they bring to your soul.

When you feel ready, concentrate once again on your breathing and become aware of your actual surroundings. Close your chakras as detailed in chapter 2 to ground and protect yourself. Take a few sips of water, and don't forget to snuff out your candle!

It is the purpose of our lives to work with angels and partner them in their work of bringing the love and wisdom of the Divine to all humankind. This is the work that our spirit yearns for and that can bring us the greatest satisfaction and reward as well as a profound healing in our own lives.

Chapter 30

REFLECTIONS

Working with angels, whether to heal our own lives or help bring healing to humankind, is work the soul readily adapts to, for partnering with angels in this way is the purpose for our being. Such work helps us find the divine spark within and thus unites us with our deepest spirit. Through working with angels, our spirit is able to manifest more and more in our personalities to bring happiness and joy and a fulfilling purpose to our lives. This purpose is what our souls are seeking, and the angels are overjoyed if just one person on earth responds, for it is amazing what one single person can achieve when working with angels. Remember, we have within us a deep spiritual power, and this power can help us achieve the most amazing things.

This power, when guided by angels, can bring healing to the world, to the animal kingdom, and, most of all, to our everyday lives. This power, which is at the heart of our being, can work miracles in our lives when we develop it with the help of the angels.

By sending the healing light of angels out into the world, you are bringing a touch of magic to the lives of many people who would otherwise never know the reality of angels. This work can open their minds to the touch of angels and increase awareness of the angelic realm that is there just waiting to be touched by human hearts.

Whatever work you choose to do from this book, rest assured that it will have a profound effect somewhere in the world, for all angel work is capable of bringing magic and joy to countless lives. You may feel that you are doing nothing, but in reality you will be achieving much. The angels will be overjoyed at your commitment, which makes their work so much more powerful and productive.

This work will also help to open your heart center chakra and put you in touch with the spark of the Divine that dwells within you. This will bring an untold joy to your soul and help you develop spiritually, something that can only bring a deep satisfaction to your soul. You will find that your life is happier and that you have a more positive outlook, and things will run more smoothly. You will attract happiness and positive things into your life, for when you are working with angels, anything can happen, and often does!

The magic of angels will indeed manifest in your life, and a subtle healing will take place regarding the problems you experience. Angels are our dearest friends and are always with us. They never desert us, even when we are at our lowest. They are there ready to lift us up and carry us through our darkest times.

Treasure the friendships and partnerships you establish with your angel work, and you will find your life transformed very much for the better. A newfound happiness will color your soul and bring to your everyday life a renewed inspiration and joy. Enjoy your work with angels, and joy will manifest in miraculous ways in your life!

ANGEL HEALING
CHECKLIST

If you want to bring healing to the world or to yourself, just call upon the angels for help. Here is a list of the different angels and archangels and the types of healing that each specializes in.

Seraphim Angels

Hierarchy: First

Choir: First

Healing Work: To send love and support to those involved
when there is some sort of disaster, whether natural or
terrorist. The healing is directed toward healing the grief
and trauma of rescue workers and victims alike.

Cherubim Angels

Hierarchy: First

Choir: Second

Healing Work: For protection when feeling threatened. If you find yourself in a negative or threatening situation and want some protection, call on the Cherubim.

To break the vicious cycle of negativity. The Cherubim bring the power and warmth of the sun to our lives to transmute lethargy and negative feelings into joyous energy and enthusiasm for life.

THRONE ANGELS

Hierarchy: First

Choir: Third

Healing Work: To heal relationship issues and bring
harmony and happiness back to your life. Thrones
will give you inspiration and ideas on how to meet
like-minded people. Working with them will bring
a purpose to your life and attract new friendships.

Dominion Angels

Hierarchy: Second

Choir: Fourth

Healing Work: To find inner wisdom. The Dominions
will help you to access the wonderful love, wisdom,
and peace of your inner spirit. They also have in their
care all religious organizations on earth, and they
bring their divine wisdom to church leaders and also
to political leaders.

Virtue Angels

Hierarchy: Second

Choir: Fifth

Healing Work: To help heal and safeguard the planet.
Virtue angels bring the light of wisdom to those in
positions of power in the world to heighten their
awareness of green issues. They have the whole earth
in their care, and they work tirelessly to heal the
planet.

To bring harmony to the world, and peace where
there is conflict. Virtues bring their healing love to
bear on world leaders where there is disharmony, war,
and conflict on a national or international scale.

Powers Angels

Hierarchy: Second

Choir: Sixth

Healing Work: To combat evil in the world. Powers angels bring forth the goodness that rests deeply in the human heart and eradicate negativity, or evil, in all its forms.

To remove negative emotional blocks that are hindering you on the spiritual path. Powers angels can help unblock the negative energy that is preventing you from moving on and bring you to a place of understanding, love, and forgiveness.

Principality Angels

Hierarchy: Third

Choir: Seventh

Healing Work: To protect endangered species. Principalities give support to all those organizations and individuals who work to protect animals. They also work on the hearts of those who poach and hunt various species and endanger their survival in the wild.

To promote human rights and eradicate discrimination. The Principality angels can bring the recognition that we are all the same beneath the ego, and there is nothing to fear.

To bring positive energy to our towns and cities. Principalities work to combat the negative energy of cities and endeavor to bring forth the positive goodness of all citizens in a creative and harmonious way.

ARCHANGEL MICHAEL

Hierarchy: Third

Choir: Eighth

Healing Work: To protect the weak and fight injustice.
Archangel Michael can help if you feel vulnerable in
some way or if you have been the victim of injustice.
His love and power can bring about a resolution and
help bring forgiveness to your heart, which is the one
sure route to positive healing.

Archangel Raphael

Hierarchy: Third

Choir: Eighth

Healing Work: To heal disease and illness, in humans and
animals. Meditation with Archangel Raphael will bring
the healing power of the Divine to your body and also
help dismiss the fear that serious illness can bring,
bringing to your heart a new confidence in your
recovery.

Archangel Uriel

Hierarchy: Third

Choir: Eighth

Healing Work: To help you find direction in life and give you the confidence to follow your dreams. Archangel Uriel will give you the courage to take steps to change your life and follow your dreams with a positive outlook.

ARCHANGEL GABRIEL

Hierarchy: Third

Choir: Eighth

Healing Work: To help you make major changes in your life with ease. Archangel Gabriel's love and power can help things run smoothly and can help you feel calm and have the strength to cope with the transition period.

To heal anxiety. Anxiety feeds on anxiety, but the power of Archangel Gabriel will give you the strength to break out of its grip and give you the courage to face your tasks and problems.

Archangel Chamuel

Hierarchy: Third

Choir: Eighth

Healing Work: For help on the spiritual path. Archangel
Chamuel will guide you and lead you to the path that
best suits your needs, and he will always be by your side
to whisper words of encouragement and inspiration.

To attract abundance and prosperity into your life.
Meditation with Archangel Chamuel will help heal any
negative beliefs you have about money and bring you
the prosperity you so richly deserve and are entitled to
as a child of the universe.

Archangel Jophiel

Hierarchy: Third

Choir: Eighth

Healing Work: To find creative inspiration and appreciation of beauty. Your life will take on a new purpose as Archangel Jophiel reveals to you latent talents and gifts that you can develop to create a more contented and beautiful life for yourself.

To heal depression. Archangel Jophiel will bring his great love to heal your soul if you feel depressed or down about something, and regular meditation with him will lift your spirits out of the darkness and bring joy to your heart once again.

ARCHANGEL RAGUEL

Hierarchy: Third

Choir: Eighth

Healing Work: To gain self-confidence. Archangel Raguel
will lift your spirits and bring a renewed hope to your
being that will encourage you to take on your tasks
with a fresh enthusiasm and lack of fear.

THE ANGELS

Hierarchy: Third

Choir: Ninth

Healing Work: For help with individual problems. Angels are the ones who give their help on an everyday basis to help us through the minor problems in our lives. Angels will also bring you messages, so always be open to thoughts and ideas that pop into your mind.

To send love into the world. When working with angels to send love into the world, you are awakening the divine spark at the center of your being, and this can have a profound effect on your life. By sending out love, you attract love and positive elements to yourself, which can only make for a better and more rewarding life.

To Write to the Author

If you wish to contact the author or would like more information about this book, please write to the author in care of Llewellyn Worldwide Ltd. and we will forward your request. Both the author and publisher appreciate hearing from you and learning of your enjoyment of this book and how it has helped you. Llewellyn Worldwide Ltd. cannot guarantee that every letter written to the author can be answered, but all will be forwarded. Please write to:

Patricia Papps
℅ Llewellyn Worldwide
2143 Wooddale Drive
Woodbury, MN 55125-2989

Please enclose a self-addressed stamped envelope for reply,
or $1.00 to cover costs. If outside the U.S.A., enclose
an international postal reply coupon.

Many of Llewellyn's authors have websites with additional information and resources. For more information, please visit our website at http://www.llewellyn.com.

GET MORE AT LLEWELLYN.COM

Visit us online to browse hundreds of our books and decks, plus sign up to receive our e-newsletters and exclusive online offers.

- **• Free tarot readings • Spell-a-Day • Moon phases**
- **• Recipes, spells, and tips • Blogs • Encyclopedia**
- **• Author interviews, articles, and upcoming events**

GET SOCIAL WITH LLEWELLYN

Find us on Facebook

www.Facebook.com/LlewellynBooks

Follow us on

twitter™

www.Twitter.com/Llewellynbooks

GET BOOKS AT LLEWELLYN

LLEWELLYN ORDERING INFORMATION

Order online: Visit our website at www.llewellyn.com to select your books and place an order on our secure server.

Order by phone:
- Call toll free within the U.S. at 1-877-NEW-WRLD (1-877-639-9753)
- Call toll free within Canada at 1-866-NEW-WRLD (1-866-639-9753)
- We accept VISA, MasterCard, and American Express

Order by mail:
Send the full price of your order (MN residents add 6.875% sales tax) in U.S. funds, plus postage and handling to: Llewellyn Worldwide, 2143 Wooddale Drive Woodbury, MN 55125-2989

POSTAGE AND HANDLING

STANDARD (U.S. & Canada):
(Please allow 12 business days)
$25.00 and under, add $4.00.
$25.01 and over, FREE SHIPPING.

INTERNATIONAL ORDERS (airmail only):
$16.00 for one book, plus $3.00 for each additional book.

Visit us online for more shipping options.
Prices subject to change.

FREE CATALOG!

To order, call
1-877-NEW-WRLD
ext. 8236
or visit our website

Messages of Hope and Healing
From Loved Ones

ANGEL

WHISPERS

MAUDY FOWLER
AND GAIL HUNT

Angel Whispers
Messages of Hope and Healing From Loved Ones
Maudy Fowler and Gail Hunt

Ever since she was eleven years old, Maudy Fowler knew she had an amazing gift: the ability to hear messages from angels. She became a mystic, delivering countless messages to individuals who seek comfort, encouragement, and hope from the angels of their deceased loved ones.

Join Maudy on an inspirational journey, featuring uplifting stories and common-sense advice on finding your life's purpose and mission. By relaying the angel messages, she calms people in crisis, reaffirms their faith in the hereafter, and encourages them to move forward. Each chapter shares the seven elements by which to live: love, honor, respect, patience, courage, forgiveness, and belief. Whether they're family, friends, or pets, *Angel Whispers* explores how angels always stay close to those they love.

978-0-7387-2783-7, 240 pp., 5³⁄₁₆ x 8   \$14.99

To order, call 1-877-NEW-WRLD
Prices subject to change without notice
Order at Llewellyn.com 24 hours a day, 7 days a week!

THE
ANGEL
CODE

*Your Interactive Guide
to Angelic Communication*

CHANTEL LYSETTE

The Angel Code

Your Interactive Guide to Angelic Communication
CHANTEL LYSETTE

Is that song on the radio a sign from heaven?

With signature sass and wit, Chantel Lysette offers a fun, hands-on program for getting in touch with your angels. She'll help you sharpen your intuitive skills, create an ideal meditation space, and open yourself to divine guidance. Get acquainted with sixteen different angels—their personalities, the feelings they evoke, how they may appear, numerous associations, and countless other clues for recognizing their presence and deciphering angelic messages. Worksheets and journal pages allow you to easily record your spiritual encounters and compile your own unique "angel code" for connecting with Gabriel, Metatron, Michael, Raphael, and other heavenly hosts.

978-0-7387-2123-1, 288 pp., 7½ x 9⅛ $17.95

To order, call 1-877-NEW-WRLD
Prices subject to change without notice
Order at Llewellyn.com 24 hours a day, 7 days a week!

Melissa Alvarez

365 Ways

*

to Raise *Your*

*

Frequency

Simple Tools to Increase
Your Spiritual Energy
for Balance, Purpose, and Joy

365 Ways to Raise Your Frequency

Simple Tools to Increase Your Spiritual Energy
for Balance, Purpose, and Joy

Melissa Alvarez

The soul's vibrational rate, our spiritual frequency, has a huge impact on our lives. As it increases, so does our capacity to calm the mind, connect with angels and spirit guides, find joy and enlightenment, and achieve what we want in life.

This simple and inspiring guide makes it easy to elevate your spiritual frequency every day. Choose from a variety of ordinary activities, such as singing and cooking. Practice visualization exercises and techniques for reducing negativity, manifesting abundance, tapping into Universal Energy, and connecting with your higher self. Discover how generous actions and a positive attitude can make a difference. You'll also find long-term projects and guidance for boosting your spiritual energy to new heights over a lifetime.

978-0-7387-2740-0, 432 pp., 5 x 7   **$16.95**

To order, call 1-877-NEW-WRLD
Prices subject to change without notice
Order at Llewellyn.com 24 hours a day, 7 days a week!

108 Practices to Live a
Divinely Inspired Life
Awake in the world
DEBRA MOFFITT

Awake in the World

108 Practices to Live a Divinely Inspired Life
DEBRA MOFFITT

Everyone needs an anchor in this fast-paced and chaotic world. *Awake in the World* offers 108 easy ways to weave soul-nourishing peace and divinity into each day.

This engaging and practical guide was inspired by the author's own personal quest for spiritual enrichment. The practices she brought back from a journey around the world changed her life—and can transform yours. Drawn from an array of wisdom traditions, these 108 bite-sized exercises—involving meditation, labyrinth walking, inspired lovemaking, mantras, and ritual—are quick and simple to do. By sharpening your spiritual awareness, you'll learn to cultivate calm in a crisis, focus on what is truly important, and recognize the divine in everyday life. To support and encourage you on this exciting journey of self-discovery, the author shares her own personal, moving stories.

978-0-7387-2722-6, 432 pp., 5 x 7　　　　　$16.95

To order, call 1-877-NEW-WRLD
Prices subject to change without notice
Order at Llewellyn.com 24 hours a day, 7 days a week!

Finding
Your Center,
Getting in the Flow,
&
Creating the Life You Desire

The Art of Bliss

Tess Whitehurst

Author of *Magical Housekeeping*

The Art of Bliss

Finding Your Center, Getting in the Flow, and Creating the Life You Desire

TESS WHITEHURST

Bring harmony and balance to every area of your life with this gentle, loving guide to beautiful living and personal evolution.

Popular author Tess Whitehurst offers a totally unique and fun magical system for reconnecting with your bliss, also known as your life force energy. Weaving together the I Ching, feng shui, and a sprinkling of magic, she teaches you to activate your nine life keys for success and happiness. Become attuned to the areas of serenity, life path, synchronicity, creativity, romance, radiance, prosperity, harmony, and synergy—and awaken each with affirmations, breathwork, prayer, meditation, smudging, rituals, and many more energetically potent tools.

978-0-7387-3196-4, 312 pp., 5³⁄₁₆ x 8 $16.99

To order, call 1-877-NEW-WRLD
Prices subject to change without notice
Order at Llewellyn.com 24 hours a day, 7 days a week!

Garden of Bliss

Cultivating the Inner Landscape
for Self-Discovery

DEBRA MOFFITT

Garden of Bliss

Cultivating the Inner Landscape for Self-Discovery
DEBRA MOFFITT

Garden of Bliss begins on the French Riviera, where Moffitt, despite her glamorous European lifestyle, is unhappy. Realizing that financial success doesn't necessarily equate to happiness, she looks inside herself and decides to make some changes.

The message of her journey is simple: bliss is a destination that exists within all of us. Using the metaphor of a secret garden, Moffitt encourages her readers to manifest this space in the physical world and connect with the divine feminine through nature. *Garden of Bliss* can be read as a stand-alone book or as a companion text to Moffitt's award-winning debut, *Awake in the World*.

978-0-7387-3382-1, 288 pp., 5³⁄₁₆ x 8 $16.99

To order, call 1-877-NEW-WRLD
Prices subject to change without notice
Order at Llewellyn.com 24 hours a day, 7 days a week!

TESS WHITEHURST

the

GOOD
ENERGY
BOOK

CREATING HARMONY AND BALANCE
FOR YOURSELF AND YOUR HOME

The Good Energy Book

Creating Harmony and Balance for Yourself and Your Home

TESS WHITEHURST

This gem of a book teaches you how to become a fountain of good energy. Discover how to maintain positive energy in your home—and establish lifelong habits and perspectives that will bring happiness and attract all good things.

Popular author and columnist Tess Whitehurst presents a holistic system for keeping your energy positive and traversing any place, situation, or challenge with confidence, clarity, and grace. She shares fun and effective techniques that draw from both the physical and energetic realms, telling you not just what to do, but also why you're doing it and even how it works.

978-0-7387-2772-1, 240 pp., 5³⁄₁₆ x 8　　　　　　**$14.95**

To order, call 1-877-NEW-WRLD
Prices subject to change without notice
Order at Llewellyn.com 24 hours a day, 7 days a week!

ENHANCE RELATIONSHIPS WITH YOUR SPIRITUAL COMPANIONS

GUIDES
guardians
AND
angels

D.J. CONWAY

Guides, Guardians and Angels

Enhance Relationships with Your Spiritual Companions

D. J. CONWAY

We may not see them. We may not hear them. But angels and spirit guides are with us all the time. Who are these entities? What is their purpose? How can we communicate with them?

Guides, Guardians and Angels is much more than an in-depth, cross-cultural exploration of these otherworldly beings. D. J. Conway reveals the role that these spiritual companions play and demonstrates how to develop a relationship with them through meditation, chants, rituals, and spells.

Take a fascinating tour of the multilayered Otherworld. Catch a glimpse of life between lives. Discover how power animals, nature spirits, dragons, light and shadow angels, and the spirits of friends, family, and pets fit into the spiritual equation. Revolutionize your understanding of Lucifer and other "fallen" angels. And learn from Conway's own personal experiences, which reinforce the profound impact these spirit teachers can have on our lives.

978-0-7387-1124-9, 192 pp., 6 x 9 $17.95

To order, call 1-877-NEW-WRLD
Prices subject to change without notice
Order at Llewellyn.com 24 hours a day, 7 days a week!

My

CONVERSATIONS

With Angels

Inspirational Moments with Guardian Spirits

Judith Marshall

My Conversations with Angels

Inspirational Moments with Guardian Spirits

JUDITH MARSHALL

All the time, including this very moment, an angel is with you. This amazing collection of true, breathtaking encounters with angels and guardians will convince you that angelic guidance, healing, and protection are truly possible.

In addition to these genuine, touching experiences from the author, her family, and her friends, this inspiring guide describes divine helpers in detail. Learn about a wide range of loving celestial beings—archangels, ascended masters, spirit guides, totem animals, and others. Discover the role they play in our lives and how to recognize their presence. There are also simple meditation techniques to help you initiate contact with angels, interpret their messages, and tap into a divine network of unconditional love and wisdom.

978-0-7387-3286-2, 240 pp., 5³⁄₁₆ x 8   **$15.99**

To order, call 1-877-NEW-WRLD
Prices subject to change without notice
Order at Llewellyn.com 24 hours a day, 7 days a week!

RICHARD HARVEY

The Inner Journey to Authenticity
& Spiritual Enlightenment

Your Essential
SELF

This book will add needed light to your journey, and help you see what only the willing heart can see.
—GUY FINLEY, international bestselling author of *The Secret of Letting Go*